Towns in the Great Desert

By the same author:

Coming Home From the World
The Blue Cloud of Crying
Acceptance of Silent Water
What the Painter Saw in Our Faces
Museum of Space
Apocrypha

Towns in the Great Desert:
New & Selected Poems

Peter Boyle

PUNCHER & WATTMANN

First published in 2013
Published by Puncher and Wattmann
PO Box 279
Waratah NSW 2298

http://www.puncherandwattmann.com

puncherandwattmann@bigpond.com

ISBN   978-1-922186-39-3 (book)
        978-1-922186-40-9 (ebook)

NATIONAL
LIBRARY
OF AUSTRALIA

A catalogue record for this book is available from the National Library of Australia

Cover design by Matthew Holt

Printed by Lightning Source International

This project has been assisted by the Australian Government through the Australia Council, its arts funding and advisory body.

Australian Government

Australia Council
for the Arts

Contents

Towns in the Great Desert (2013)

(New Poems 2009 – 2013)

I Towns in the Great Desert

II

III Nightpoems

IV

Selected Poems   (1988 – 2009)

From "Coming home from the world" (1994)

from "The Blue Cloud of Crying" (1997)

from "What the painter saw in our faces" (2001)

from "Museum of Space" (2004)

from "Reading Borges" (2007)

from "Apocrypha" (2009)

I
Towns In The Great Desert

Towns in the Great Desert (1)

The frozen river zigzags through the many-layered city.
Stranded cars sleep moored to old boats
rusted into landmarks.
She wakes from a dream of pounding doors,
her head racing like a wired alarm clock.
She walks through the house, naming the chairs
while a neighbour's cat
purrs in imagined kinship.
If you climb down into the snow,
a bird on a windowsill says,
you will find the sun is waiting there too.

A fine wind blows over the ice.
At a corner where
two streets face the end of explanations,
a small boy squats to collect ants.
Just now he's noticed how
the shells of ants
are crackling with inner fire.

Night serves a writ against travellers.
A woman arrives with two children asleep in a matchbox.
She unwraps the linen that binds their limbs
and places them side by side
on the mantelpiece.
Soon a small tree
is curving the memory of forests
over their unwritten faces.

Towns in the Great Desert (2)

The size of tall-masted ships,
of a spire of prayer,
the gate of hammered earth
and nailed wooden planks
is wheeled shut at second watch.
Guards wield huge feral dogs on iron chains
while other dogs laze about unchained
to supervise late arrivals.

The last to make his way through the closing gates,
he drags himself with the stumps of his arms,
battered legs trailing over stony ground.
Each night he sleeps in an old car,
turns the motor to a slow hum, climbs
into the engine, curls up beside its warmth,
locks the bonnet behind him.
His skin at dawn has the black fragrance of oil.
Each day he stretches out on the beach
to be pounded clean by the surf.
His body has the purple glow
of finely tuned mallets.

In the sky of this town there are no passing clouds or stars,
only the unbroken wall of millennial dust.
Sea water is all there is
to cook, to bathe, to wash.
To buy water to drink
they send their children to slave in distant mines.
Of this town they say
"The gods never came here."

Towns in the Great Desert (3)

The world has been divided many times over
yet no one has claimed ownership
of this wandering undecided mirage.
On a dry riverbed
a fleet of boats chained to the bones of the earth:
such is our town.
A busload of tourists arrive, drink coffee
on the steps of their bus
and argue the omnipotence of maps.

Two armies camp here —
each is hiding from a different war.
Scraping a ladle across sand
a mother spells out the saga of the stars
in unsacred glyphs.
The sliding planets
point to the lines
on the withered hands of our children.

Going nowhere is the art of our navigators.

Towns in the Great Desert (4)

Vertical town,
once home to the growers of bananas
and children who never knew twilight.
On every level of this town
performers astound the easily distracted desert breezes.
An artificial waterfall types letters.
A young girl has invented flowers that talk.
By popular request
a boxed doctor from Bologna
performs exhumations on the hour.

Above the deep ravine of a riverbed,
suspended from wayward anti-gravity balloons,
this city floats at the precise distance
best suited for harvesting potential raindrops.
Some smuggle oxygen inside their spines,
others attempt the fabrication of ersatz moisture.
Only the rich are privileged to know
the taste of water.

At the summit of the vertical city
a many-layered supermarket
where the poor trade
the pre-sold equity of their bones
for boxes with the names of exotic foods,
clothes, landscapes, narratival machines.
Scanning in barcodes, they watch on giant screens
what their lives might have been
if the rains had come,
if containers weren't all empty.

Towns in the Great Desert (5)

Arrived here from the outside
you stop in wonder:
lights swaying in tall
honeycombs of glass.
Against the starless sky
seen across the flat dark water
these shells of lives lit up from the inside
exposed at random, so close, almost touchable.

Behind the transparency of glass
the lights spell something you cannot name
as if a summons from somewhere inside yourself
you have never travelled to,
as if here you could begin again.
Snow falls into your hands.
You stand watching in a small square
where a golden tree goes on defying winter.
A woman on a caged balcony
releases a dove into the frozen desert wind.
In a cubicle made of light
two men unpack a box
filled with stones.

Towns in the Great Desert (6)

They have built their parallel town
on the plateau of the clouds.
The patchwork of ladders
has at last found firm foundation.
Meticulously
they have dragged everything with them –
tarpaulins, cardboard boxes, tin sheets, old car-frames---
to establish the first favela of the clouds.
They have rigged up their TV sets
to the random migration of lightning.
Lounging in deckchairs, like elegant movie stars,
they sip all day
on a fine distillation of water vapour.
Meanwhile, stung by sudden jealousy, the rich
go by in planes that look like oversized tourist buses.

Most of all, to this undulating
plateau of spun clouds
they have brought their dead in wooden boxes.
What could never find place on earth
is safely at home here.
When the desert dwellers below
think the sky is groaning under the heavy weight of cloudbanks
it's no trick of the wind, no clinking in the wheels
of the enormous sky factory
that reprocesses salt.

Peacefully far above us
the dead are snoring.

Towns in the Great Desert (7)

There are so many steps you must navigate
to reach the quiet core of the earth.
You stand in a room and call out
but no sound comes.
Sleep has grown all around you
like a beautiful plant.
A confused nuggetty man
is fumbling a mug of raw cinders.
He hands you an ancient rare-edition guidebook
for the town you plan to construct
if you could only sleep long enough.
At the core of the earth
he has put on your sweater and you can't understand
why monsters keep peeling off you
like self-generating wallpaper.
All that moss with its green tangle of pseudo-grass
voraciously feeding on sunlessness.

The centre of the earth you travel to each night
is a small inkling of how it is
when life closes over.
Raw puddle
of a lone waterdrop.
In your slowly opening hand
the wired ancestry of stars:

from the accident of all accidents
these breaths
fated and numbered.

Towns in the Great Desert (8)

"Green Ocean Resort Hotel" the sign reads.
Here in the centre of a wide flat plain
a line of deckchairs wait
for the millennial arrival of waves.
Among crumbling skeletons of desert birds,
the wind-blown grit of dust from disused
chalk mines, rotted freeways, oases of styrofoam,
I await the palm trees,
I await the sky lifting summer off the plain.

Here
where no water has been seen for a thousand years
they erect a shark observation deck
and paint directions for balloons to stop
bringing tourists from remote sunken cities
as they draw the character for water,
for its flowing presence,
the shifting abundance of its rippling
under stars,

and I dream the arrival of the great fleet,
lost fishing boats,
the trawlers of the seven skies,
while the earth is an immense open hand
bearing the stamp of the prayer for water
inscribed into the cancer of its bones.

Towns in the Great Desert (9)

Hovering always between modernity and decrepitude
the sky-scraper jostles its way
through the low-lying clouds.
Already the habitat of disconnected wires,
the ground floor boarded up,
its cracked glass taped, the carpet
drizzled in dog-piss, while far above
the casino, revolving restaurant and Penthouse
blaze and creak in ill-omened
oceanic winds.
Each day the citizens of this town
swap uniforms from millionaire to hobo.

In the canals, sharks cruise,
frenzied by toxic run-off.
Speculators in eroded land
subdivide the air between the buildings.
The punters await the Sky God
in thongs and T-shirt.
In the slot machines on each corner
fluted glasses of champagne
await trembling hands.
By five a.m. the shoes of the all-night dancers
find their way to the end of long jetties
from where they can dive
into the blue-grey ice of no-memory.

Hard-wired to adolescence,
at thirty the people of this town return
to being aged twelve.

Everywhere
the gold-haired bright-eyed faces
tilt coyly to watch themselves
being watched on television
while, all around,
sullen casinos go on with the quiet task
of redistributing emptiness.

Towns in the Great Desert (10)

It is the hour.
The termites have crawled into the piano.
A pelican swoops low overhead.
At the crossroads my long-dead unborn brother
is stalled at the mercy of traffic,
this everywhere ghost
come out of the skies.
Before me
a spiral of cracked bitumen
spins faster and faster
and on board whirling pedestrians, time travellers,
each clutching, like a magical umbrella,
the expressionless stare of their identity card.

When the spiral stops,
myself walking backwards, stark naked,
I am inside a picture-book Chinatown
where all the signs are painted
not just on swaying lanterns
but on my body and somewhere deep
inside myself.
At the fruit stall they pluck onions from my navel.
At the beauty parlour they will remake my head.

Waking up Chinese
I decipher the ideograms
on the herbalist's half-open door:
"*town that steps across time*
to be both now and vanished".

The rain goes on entering me:
one long remorseless blessing.
I am ground ginger in the apothecary's bowl.
The desert blooms from every fracture of my bones.

Towns in the Great Desert (11)

What mattered most in the dream
was the quality of blue in the water
so that it wasn't about the naked young man, my rival,
doing handstands and backflips into the canal
or any wince of pain from contemplating in reverse image
the hammered remnants of my own body.
Like the perfect alignment of sailboats on a blue sea,
between the world and the world
the canal made a corridor
for whales and the white refuse of icebergs
to drift between familiar department stores,
the takeaway, the news-stand and the corner pub.
Suddenly how far away from death I was,
standing alone and speechless
before the waters of the sky,
this proof
that the depths go on shining.

II

The Tree's Ambition

A tree with the deep ambition of becoming an ant: long evenings in night school, first attempts at rapid movement, countless resits of *Thinking like a team* (Business Studies 5071).

One day the tree realises: becoming an ant requires the perfection of smallness. The tree would start by concentrating its being in a single leaf, a dry leaf, preferably, scored with old wounds. Next it would work on narrowing its life span, ideally to no more than a few intense hours.

The tree thinks: living like an ant means living inside death – so much industry, endless conferences on collaboration, decisions taken in microseconds. Death as a name for a species, a destiny.

Here, inside its bark, watching a tribe of ants, unable to join their purposive non-stop rush hour. The sadness of being a tree. Its branches fall back around it like a song of defeat. "Farewell boys, comrades of my dreams, I must sleep with my silence. Always trying to mouth the one green syllable, condemned to the dunce's chair. Me and my eternal shadow. My inability to organize a planet."

Crow

(in memory of Val Plumwood)

The sound of crows is known to us for its mournfulness, its insistent black edge to a bright world. There was a day when she stepped into a clearing and surprised crows at their other speech, the cheerful joyous rapture they know from time to time when no one is about, when they are completely free of all other creatures' expectations. It did not last long, less than a minute, before the crows perceived her startled presence. In that minute how taken home she felt to the world's deep joy.

Coda:

Or perhaps as a girl what had happened was this: for one moment she became a crow and heard crows the way crows hear themselves. Nothing has changed in the singing of the crows, the same pitches and frequencies spliced against a clearing in sunlight. Only for this one time her ears, her entire being, perceived these sounds according to the delicate inner coding of a crow. Just like the small brown and grey birds, so drab to our eyes, that to each other are splashes of the brightest iridescent colour, so, through a strange grace, she had perceived that day for those few moments as a crow does, had grasped their smooth eloquent harmonies gliding between the interrupted stuttering of the trees.

Fig Tree

The fig tree in autumn laments its journey to the sun. All that distance it has travelled to find warmth and now reluctantly it feels itself sent back, plodding those interminable miles and the view across the river and the pile of abandoned cars, now three or four, now five or six, only minor variations on the topos abandonment. With a touch of exhaustion it shrugs off its regrets. Maybe one day, it mutters, and then there are still the birds whose chatter, almost intelligible, reminds him how chirpy some people can feel. The sun, yes, one day he will go back there. One day, yes, that fire in the bones.

Calendulas

In winter I am an old man, naked and in socks,
sprinting through the birches of Scandinavia.

In spring I am a young girl watching wisteria blossom at the edge of a well:
dark water is breaking through fissures in the earth,
my breath discovers I am the child of mud.

They beat me with iron and rope,
a blue winding sheet covers my limbs,
they take the white lines from my body and process maps of the stars.

In summer I am a woman with five children, a shepherd of the ocean
that comes to play in the backyard
under the withering leaves of laundry,
under fire's azure death-banner.

In autumn I am the accountant of a million bus tickets gathered
from a world that has taken off to visit the sky.

A crack in a vase,
a break in a wall
that opens on spinning silence,
a whirlwind of dust.
They vaporize me,
they conscript me into smoke.

On Easter Monday I am the sister who comes out of the grave,
takes a cab home, collects all her childhood
and walks back, singing riffs from old psalms,
into the smooth history of the river.

On the Day of the Dead I am stone, a jug of aguardiente,
a vase of purple messengers
solemnly chanting the rabbit's genealogy.

On the day of the Equinox I am the fish that takes the golden balance
of moist and dry, fire and snow,
hunger and fear and ecstasy,
back to the ocean's floor.

A stash of tobacco
folded inside my socks,
a snapped finger that knows
the truth of all hands,
they have nailed my tongue
back into my viscera,
they splinter me, they exorcise my memory.

On the Day of All Births I am a small voice opening a window to the sun.

Reading Max Jacob in Taichung

for Philip Hammial

«La terre entière brûlera" (*Folklore 1943*)

What is it that one writes to the very end and how does one write it?

All day a sulphurous smoke moves across the construction sites. One imagines air and water laced forever with the thin-spun fire of vast turbines that grind the mountains into dust.

He wanders through a Paris of tour guides and monuments, of bishops and dignitaries, everywhere the old graceful formalities, the allure of progress, peace and serenity, the bureaucratic flow of language asserting the golden age, and always at street corners the bronze sound-chambers of wells, dark fountains of water from which rise, regular and echoing, the screams of hell. Attempting invisibility, he glides between two-legged wolves who wear the masks of company managers, consultants on urban renewal, police chiefs and advisers on the purification of air. Small stars made from coughed venom spin like shiny barbs down the gutters that run at all times under our feet. Shrinking to the size of a new-born child, he glides between the monsters and the monsters, carrying inside him a round loaf of bread that has blazed and will blaze before and after our species.

Max Jacob in the last days before Drancy, I imagine one universal yellow star.

Sierra Madre

The mother mountains,
how thin and tall they are –
ancient and wiry,
hunched over streams
endlessly scaling fish.

The withered nipples
their fingers gesture towards –
what lips will touch them now
and the spot that life came from,
how carefully they tuck the skirts of rock in there
that the sun
should not peer through.

Washing the feet of wilful children,
they serve snow
in small bowls of leaves.
They say
"tell me a story".

The mother mountains
see further than the stars.
They have no need
to travel the earth.

How could I love,
who have never loved,
the chill grey sparkle of eyes
ash-glow in the rounded hollow
of caves?

Delicately shrunken to gaunt bones,
how can I carry the mountains?
How can I lift
and tenderly fold them
to their final rest?

Berlin-Buch, August 2009

Falling asleep in a hospital in Germany
is like dozing fully clothed and awake
among the crowds of the dead.
I saw caves painted with bison, saw
masks and figures on trains, sat beside
fat ladies and men wearing teeth, rattled
through a fairground like a baited bear, and men
in pelts of foxes and wolves
held out arrows towards me
and I understood how the fish were running
in the streams. There was a bell ringing
on a train where I sat packed in
between schoolgirls and sausages.
I said to myself, of course I am asleep
and there is safety in being only a passenger
and then a man from some tribe five thousand years ago
ran his fingers along my shoulder, a gob of congealed
cow-blood planting the sign of the ox
on my smallpox scar.
I understood I might have been invited
to a wedding that took place
in a field where my bed lies
sometime when small people in boats
were crossing the lakes out of Africa
and fire would break at odd moments
from their fingers, stealing light
from the sky's lower stars.
In my right hand
a patched scar has quilted a sign
for the late summer swallows —

the scar in the palm of my right hand
is a long sequence of crossroads
going back to the invention of axes.
"Do you want to go with us far into the forests?"
I understood some hunters were willing to take me
across the hills into Asia,
perhaps we would search out those secret tunnels
that transmitted pollen from the earth's first spring
between Iceland and China.

Then the carriage jolts again,
this steel-framed casing where my body is transported
between whatever decrees have been issued for its fate.
So many people pierce me with their eyes.
From a corner window seat
I see the dizzying chronicle of my births
and, when the train slows,
just beyond the eastern suburbs of Berlin
a lake comes into view,
a low riverbank and, eloquent
as a stone path entering the sky, a turtle
has just left its log.
The fragile constellation of its face
welcomes me back.

Summer Day

(reading a Cuban poem while waiting at the pathologist)

Not words on a page
but an old man opposite me
who is whispering –
his life, the furniture, the stars,
the kitchen clatter, all
appear in the air around him as he talks,
this voice that touches each thing
to verify exactly where it stands.
The tropic sun is bright and all-consuming
inside and outside the poem.
It is quiet enough to recognise his voice quite clearly.
I too am dying.
Beyond the circle of his speech
one undivided silence sustains and engulfs me:
the summer sky, Cuba walking on across the page, my suspect blood.

(an afternoon with you)

glitters in every dull or dazzling
variation of light
can be hidden discretely
in the heart of a whirlwind
worn in all weathers
valid in all jurisdictions
stays kosher in the most chaotic kitchen
minimalises all maximalists
maximises all minimalists
unites reindeer into passionate prayer circles
heals all wounds with one affordable bi-weekly
                    (or monthly) donation

raises up seashells from the Mariana Trench
humbles your average ninety-course banquet
                    on the slopes of Mt Everest
is not given in the signs of the sky
escapes the manual on the good governance of medium
                    to small kingdoms

is what
it is when
it is

for us alone
in the songbook of
our death

these vast perfections

Evening at the Diner, Hilo, Hawaii

The people in the booth opposite
seem dwarfed by the small mountains of stodge –
eggs, ham, bacon, pickles
atop macaroni-potato salad, gravy, a lava flow
of French fries.
Steadily, like hand-held cranes,
their forks scoop it up.
My father, forty-five years ago,
would talk for hours
of the wonders of American diners:
the endless cups of coffee, the smiling waitresses,
the sumptuous satisfying helpings.

All these years later,
older than my father was then,
I sit in a booth in an American diner.
Aimlessly I pick with my fork
at a double-layered Turkey sandwich
still half buried in French fries.
The waitresses are older than in the movies
but their pained smiles reach through.
As I get up
to make my way to the counter and pay
I see my father
in a booth at the far end
beaming at the wealth
of pancakes and ice cream and chocolate topping –
then, at once, it feels
I am carrying him within me.
All the way to the cashier's counter

his eyes, held back within me,
stare out into the room.
My father's boundless confidence
and his lifelong sadness
are saying farewell
to the American diner.

To a Day in October

Jar of jam resting on the balcony table at breakfast
grant sweetness to this day.

Indian mynah that hunts whatever crumbs are left on the sunstruck
        balcony
grant the gold of your beak, your always-focussed eyes.

Mysterious tree that soars from condemned earth
grant your ability to send all poison to a single leaf.

Darkening wall of the collapsing body
let light stream through every ragged chink.

Guardian angel of catastrophe
clarity as I vanish.

In the Age of Restoration

The Emperor Hirohito is being reborn
inside the dome of St Paul's Cathedral,
wearing a top hat and monocle,
swathed in umbilical bandages, hatched from an egg –
tensely the operation proceeds:
listen, the assistant says,
the silence is ending.
A purred group of words in English
murmurs like a bee-swarm on the Emperor's lips
(at birth he is already thirty)
and softly the dazzled spring leaves of London
are bowing in obeisance,
barges on the Thames
are sliding from their moorings,
storks and swallows mass in grey hushed
lines of reverence along the rooftops of the city
while his subjects – the inhabitants
of all wandering islands, great or small –
dither or dally at the usual
tasks of daylight
like a world of tiny life-worn hands
folding and unfolding their anxieties
before a great boulder descends.

The Storyteller's Cure

For twelve nights he lay awake till, at last, the storyteller was summoned

"There was once a thief no thicker than a rose's stem"

Sharp specks of a dazzling black flower infiltrated his skin

The chrysalis of the sky surrounded him

He lay beside the storyteller

The earth they would enter had already been prepared

An apple on a table, a row of dots abandoning an exercise book, a
microscope caressing dead cells all night as a swollen clock inspects
the laboratory

Water like strips of torn paper, a lizard, a door in a forest and behind it
lavender and mint

In the upturned cup of a flower, the same ocean as at the earth's end

Pebble

Accepting, rejecting the sun,
toying with its presence,
letting the sun's warm hand stretch all the way
along its flat rounded surface
yet in its own depths
what knowledge of ice ages and the steady
gathering of a million cousins
whispering in unison,
what compact silence
that feels no need to set down roots.

The sun goes on with its projects:
its cheerful face always
poking out from green foliage,
wind-etched rivers, wavebreak and rockpool.
A black fierce eye
withholds consent.

An Everyday Event

Night.
A cobbled street where a lighted door is left open.
Glints of light off the road
block all exits.
The stars and the moon are laying siege
to a house in the 12th arrondissement.
They have sectioned off the roadway,
established a no-fly zone
over the rooves.
Using tweezers
they have inserted tiny worms
in the brains of sleeping children.
Carefully they have lowered a ladder of light
that will stretch from the basement
to a shower cubicle perched on the roof.
Five families in the one house,
all have stumbled
under the scrutiny of the stars.
If any explanation is required
ask the cobblestones glimmering numbly
in their bed of sleet.
The rain of 2 a.m.
goes below the eyes
to penetrate whatever is written deep
in the bones of the forehead.

No directions from above,
no instructions from God or the cosmos –
only this strict adherence
to the random right to strip bare,

to eradicate with no sound,
no feather falling.

Everyone wakes as if nothing has happened –
only this taste like burnt wire
at the back of the throat.
A certain mental vagueness.
In the vast sea far from any land
a few more drops of extinction.

Seven Aubades

A snail recounts its experience of dawn

Like the glittering droplets of my wake, the shadow of my house has enveloped the world.

Train station at dawn

The pine forest has drawn close: a haze of pink cloud stretches my windows awake.

In the hospital ward

All night I was waiting for dawn: now I can start to relearn my ignorance of the grace hidden in waiting.

Shoes at the doorstep: daybreak

Freed from all the comings and goings we have known, we are flooded by our own openness.

Bridges at sunrise

All through the night we have held a watery chaos under our sway: now we are again a small locked door in an endless passageway, a failed mirror hung between two infinities.

A foot interrogates dawn

Why do you grow so slowly, so insistently, from far hills and treetops to the foot of this bed? Why do you waste all your light on forest paths and bending roads that can't alter our journey to death?

The birds at daybreak

Don't ask us to be your interpreters: don't come to us with your theories of night and its terrors: making the present is what we do.

Counselling the Recalcitrant

They have prepared my grave
and a box to house me.
I keep protesting the timing isn't right,
that some basic error's botched the instructions.
Their looks tell me
I've really lost the plot.
"Haven't you wondered why you keep shifting objects
and they go back to the same place,
why you scribble all day in your notebook
and none of the ink is visible?"

Exasperated,
taking me by the hand now,
they try to spell it out:
"There isn't room enough on this planet for the dead.
You can't expect to stay here as a voice in a room
rattling on and on,
as some disembodied mental spasm
that can't lift a cup, can't turn a doorhandle."

The Small Grey and Brown Birds That Recite the Lost Books of Dante

(Blue Mountains Interlude – for Hollis and Jon)

Almost inaudible at first,
they are the wind's quivering
along some country backstreet
where rows of low shrubs
shelter the earth from frost.
Their diffident chittering
lets us locate them in the attendant foliage
just outside the gates that lead
to Hell or Heaven.
Suspicious of soaring like eagles
or glowering under dark cloaks like ravens,
no penitents these, their plainness
transcending plain-chant.
In the rapt instant where they dwell
between hard earth and the highest tangle of trees
they transmit Dante's book of the eternal present
with its lines that curve to the upward beat
of thoroughly investigatory beaks – just listen
as the speckled rarity of each moment
cascades in a wavering delicate sing-song,
a counter-sonority
of pure inflection.

Snow has long covered the libraries where
the lost books spoke
in their canticles of bliss upon this earth.
One long late autumn afternoon,

curious at the white tattered specks
that fall around them,
hopping over the tracks
beyond the street's abrupt end,
these birds
inhabited by an unpredictable music.
Whatever survives
belongs to their wisdom.

New Year, 2009

Among the divided mountains only a very few
slip within the edges of our lives. Of one or two at most
can we say it was there
a certain day, a certain hour when the horizon
opened a narrow break in the unending cloudbank
or the water's interrupted mirroring
left in our eyes a sense
of that white stillness.

Only so much can be taken on trust –
the return of seasons, the chance that not every hope
is an illusion and, for today,
the great triangular mountains where the dead go,
a grey and gold-beaked bird
from somewhere near those mountains
savaging the last drops of nectar in the bottlebrush plant
on the veranda this morning.

Green Island, Taiwan

Falling asleep on a small low island
so far from any mainland
is like preparing for death.
One day it rose out of sea,
one day it will return to it.
Low wind-blown tangle of greenery,
dark volcanic rock carved by wind,
deer on the slopes of the single spine of mountains.
Here phones die out, power generators
stutter to a halt
and always the sea, the sea.
And one morning a blue fresh shift of air
rising within me.

Deep sleep of the island, this island sleep,
like seaweed, like the drumming of waves,
like the deep-cut channel of the harbour
where an anchor thrown off the deck of a fishing trawler
goes down forever
lodging me further and further
under the porous layers of the earth,
myself a transmigrating butterfly,
an earthworm, an exploding head
of pollen filaments,
this small shell of an island
lodged out in mid-ocean
in the part of the earth
that lies closest to dawn.

III
Nightpoems

Nocturne (1)

The powerful owl calls and responds across the jagged valley:
the river has just entered its being —
glittering white light of burning water —
I lie awake listening to traffic explode, a slow burning skyrocket —
I write in darkness across illegible paper —
my daughter writes stories
in another room of this house
that is all our houses —
at this hour my father and mother
drift from dream to dream in their
unjoined identical sleep-places of nowhere —
who is tapping at the fourth pane
along the glass wall guarding the valley? —
the trees are rising over the earth — blurred crowns —
a dark rooster — tonight each one
is travelling its own space

the stars only remain as a faint
shining within the wall of ghost clouds

Climbing the stairwell my daughter
already looks out over the whole village —
the stupas with their prayer flags,
the white rooftops where clothing
beats out its own life-story against
the freezing knives of the dark goddess —
here the nightly saga of the cars
along the freeway is joining remote cities —
I crouch in the cold of winter three a.m.
words slow down

and my pen finds its own way across darkness

The river has gone back to flowing

Nocturne (2)

Tonight there is no one else in the house. Birdless treeless night. When the walls collapse I walk out along a pier built into the river below in the valley. A young boy from a century ago stands there waiting for someone to turn up with a crate of beer. I walk back through the house. In the ground far underneath me I can hear the foundations of water shifting. Maybe the boy waiting for beer will find this place, will surface painfully between the slabs in the laundry and shake off his robes of humus like an earthworm spending a sleepless night inspecting a hill.

Under the earth I can hear the clanking of cables, the realignment of tunnels. A city moves by underneath. I walk through the chaos of branches that have been cleared to create the emptiness that is the house. I taste its elusive flavour: the bark, buds, roots working their way through the soil, the dissolved soap, used cups, sweat on clothes, voices taken back. On the kitchen workbench, vegetables wait patiently to be chopped.

Under a light-bulb I stand in the memory of light.

Nocturne (3)

In all the slow dignity of its days
the house steps down into the lake –
gingerly its brick walls and polished floorboards
lap the clear liquid of the sky.
The house enters among
the quietly circling fish,
the place of cormorants and herons,
the rise and tilt of moon mirrored on water
and our voices, strangely awakened in the vastness of space,
echo across fields of drifting marram grass.

In the kitchen of the house
breakfast goes on being made over and over.
Croissants burnt once on the griller
go on scenting the house –
the rescued remnants smeared with jam and butter –
and the children hunched impatiently
can only be seen from the back
always leaving.

Nocturne (4)

A single tree goes on glittering in the valley.
Five horses stop by the leaf-mulch of its base.
Dawn is a grey shiver broken by birdsong.

In the high house
above the gully of ferns and tangled scrub
my parents drift from dream to dream:
it is not yet their hour to be born.
A long dirt path meanders through bracken and tall gums –
it is my forebears, some roughneck Irish tear-aways
looking for gold, for a fabled valley of gold
and they stop in bone-freezing mist
in the chill grey uplands of Victoria,
just past mid-winter, and look:

brilliant dazzle of fairy weaving, delicate thick
bunching of blossom
soaring between twisted gums:
an explosion of gold
the wattle tree has migrated
to the slope outside my bedroom window.
In the few moments of first dawn
this golden stencil-work
filled with earth's inscriptions –
from within,
at once and forever,
light-transfigured.

The Prodigal Son

Everywhere I am finding pieces of writing called "The Prodigal Son". They are turning up in anthologies of Chinese poetry, in essays by late nineteenth century makers of almanacs, in the short stories of incarcerated romantics and accountants with a taste for an alter ego. Remorselessly I ply my way through their confessions, through the pitiful tomes of their pig farms and squandered debaucheries. All this longing for a lost path, a light in a window, the family dog grown old at the threshold. I slip in with them through the jarring bang of the fly-wire screen door, glide down the hallway between bedrooms, look out the bay window across the harbour. My parents, still overwhelming, imbalanced, father shouting, mother gone white faced, drift in outline across the kitchen, invisibly mended in the respective fifth and second years of their death. Speech and recognition are now impossible. Who are these impostors? That is when I realise my father has moved on to a lumber camp out in the Alaskan forests while my mother remains as part of me as the scar in my right hand, hovering always near, the guardian angel of catastrophe.

False Memories

The nightmare of eternal school returned to him like a thousand candles spattering a steady rain of wax across his exposed arm. A pencil, snapped off, had long ago drilled into his open hand the insignia of the scribe. Nonsense babbling at his lips and the unrelenting consciousness of being every moment under judgement were tied to his feet, like an acrobat always dragging at his heels the island he wants to escape. Between a prison and a prison he chose the one with the smaller knives. Yet he remembered (in a false memory) how Moritz Schlick was murdered by the repeated blows of sharpened pens.

Beautiful Landscape with Menace

Ahead stretches the road, there is no limit to it. Above it, leans a line of wind-cracked trees tottering on their stems; below, a pale river zigzags aimlessly, lit up by the shimmer of delicately-etched sharks, patient recyclers of our dreams.

Clarity of the Word

to cut; to run; to stay in a burrow underground; to impersonate a tree in autumn; to approach the world with an open heart and an infinite capacity for disappointment; *nm* rapturous dismay; joyful ingratitude; *nf* a type of boxing match used for divination or to contact the dead; a woman who lives off the immoral earnings of more than three husbands; (*S Am*) a pitchfork with an angel's heart; as in (*Cu*) the termites have crawled into the piano, or (*DR*) he who drinks the sea must nurse the oyster; (*RPL, Chi*) unworthy of entering a shopping mall even in a cyclone; (*Per, Ec*) gifted with fingers small enough to befriend dustmites; (*Mex, Col, Ven*) not to be trusted, not to be believed, also patron saint of fish; (as a colour) yellow, orange, red or brown; (*ornith.*) a seabird with golden wings and hard onyx beak or a small bird afraid of swamps seen only during ill-omened festivities; from Arabic, a tree that befriends doomed travellers; also see medieval Latin, a table for unwritten books; (*colloq.*) to succeed, to fail, to cough, to lose one's way etc.

Nocturne (5)

She was standing at the end of the bed
and I wanted to talk to her
but the words had to travel so far
not just from my stomach
not just through the stitches they inserted
to keep my throat
attached to my toes.
The history of damage stepped in
before the first sound-bubble broke loose
and already her smile,
that look of knowing it all,
the clear gaze of her standing there
in the blue dress at the foot of the bed,
was going, peeled
off the spinning light
like a worn plaster.

Nocturne (6)

A few more moments I thought and I would find my own way down through the cascading waterfall of the world. Every line, every breath would guide me till I found my true place on earth – allotted soil like the stand of trees outside my window in the blaze of transparent night. I listen as the cars go by weaving their temple of sound – the stars lost behind cloudbank.

Perhaps my self has already left the bed and taken on its new being at the knotted juncture of branches, inside the heart of a tree – not the tree's soul or spirit, just the ghost of myself inside the mind of the tree.

And now I set out to return. Walking tentatively on air, I travel with eyes closed, knowing how my pen (with some errors) travels the way of the dark, trusting in its free-fall, cut loose from light's security and all ruled margins. Truly in the white flesh of the eucalypt's bark I have come down to earth.

Nocturne (7)

I get lost.
In the space between
the first and last
button of my shirt
I get lost.
A shoelace is unravelling.
Rising to investigate,
one leg wants to follow the other
but I get lost.
The house, a lumbering plane,
moves towards the beckoning tarmac
as where I am slides across sixty years.
My right hand races on across the page
while my left hand goes back
to tour each room,
brushing the rows of candles into silence.
Midsummer heat. I sweat before a curling
wreath of steam.
Outside the window
a mirror suspended beside a fountain:
small wind-blown cameos.
I am right there
among all that is joined
and all that is shattered.
Into this streaming of light
(my mother
ushering me into her presence)
humbly lost.

Nocturne (8)

"Take me to the black woods mumma
and make believe we'll boogy in the dark."

In the late summer of anxiety
in the blink of a damaged left eye
a poem appears to have written itself
on a blank page
by moonlight.
A woman is crouched over the page,
her heavy rocking presence
sealing her into
the space where all is clear.
The squared lines are still just visible
as down the channels of the world
the waves roll in.
Somewhere beyond all windows
it is over.

Märchen

"There was once a Margrave of Min
who was required to bury a pin."

They stood at the edge of the last great forest, a place of tangled foliage and tall lichen-covered trees that stretched all the way to the ice sea of the North. Neuberg had expanded and expanded since the years of the catastrophe. Wherever the remnants had come together, there were the grey metallic rooves, the new ring roads and periphériques, the urban conglomerations sheltering those left after the disaster.

"You all know how it ends?" The oldest boy's voice towered above them all but especially above Felix, the newcomer.

"Of hay there was nix
not a stone or a stick
and the earth was hard rock
that gave out painful shocks
so he buried the pin
in his shin.

"But do you know what happened next?" the boy fixed his gaze at Felix for a moment, then assuming a matter-of-fact air continued:

"Oh, the pin was in his shin a long time till quite suddenly, a winter morning just like this one, he turned into a pin. First his nose turned to metal, then the rest of him twisted and wrenched, first his arms adhering to his torso, then the whole buckling into a circle, and the scream, the scream, that was the main thing. The scream is all around us in this forest, especially right here."

And, at those words, Felix heard a high-pitched wail break the limits of the sky as the older boy thrust a pin into Felix's upper right thigh. Then he saw it: the glimmer of metal on the boy's protruding teeth and a dull echo of verdigris, the tarnished mildew of copper, in his eyes.

Nocturne (9)

Zoologically we have been slowly inundated with elephants –
first in my partner's dreams, then in
my own auto-babble under the ether.
If I am to be extinguished like a fly
against the rough arse of the world,
why do elephants interpose themselves as my jovial saviours?
Their signs have followed me around for days
even before the accident.
Before the scrambling of the planets
I remember the fire of weeping
that rippled over the world
and then, interrupting the drone of disconsolate owls
and some interminable cicada,
the snorting of an elephant there
outside the window.
Has it swum here?
Did it come from the island of Elephanta?
Sounding its little trumpet a few days after my birthday
as if to tell me (despite the dizziness, the general brain fuzz)
just keep going.

A Box of Stones

They were bringing a box of stones in from the forest when some moss on the back of an old man's hand began to sing in Estonian. Here on soil that has rejoined the polar wastes, Siberian elephants and their accompanying hermaphroditic elephant tamers slog the same circle of immense frozen footsteps, bearing aloft helmets with bleeding holes where the eyes should be.

Now, as snow blankets the suburbs, I step inside a vast railway station waiting for the lights to go on. There are no booths to buy tickets and no passengers. No one is waiting for the arrival of the long-lost cousin from Patagonia. Around that time I remember it is my last night on earth and I am there, my outstretched hands touching the looping iron rail of the centuries. Spiraling domes of midsummer ice. A whirlwind of leaves has followed me inside as if they had always wanted to perform some surreal ballet of the station concourse, one last promenade over the platforms, the deserted stalls for hotdogs and late papers.

If a sad warrior appears in the palm of the hand it means a journey where every turn will remove you from yourself, ill-omened as a bat in a barbershop. That night when the trans-Siberian shift placed Sydney somewhere near Omsk and it was possible to walk south backwards, stone by stone, all the way to Norway.

Nocturne (10)

A clattering sound echoes around me like prayer wheels set spinning by the sudden brushing of wings or the fingers of ghosts. The spirit says to me, "You have three days in which you are completely free to move wherever you like. Only your body must stay here – it is under our custody, our surveillance, so it will be strapped and wired into this bed." "But how can I move if my body has to stay here?" "You will work out ways", the spirit says.

A first try and I find I'm moving along the corridor past the wards, about to enter an overpass I never knew existed above Macquarie Street and Martin Place. For a moment, remembering something essential, I return.

"But my daughter comes here to the bedside every day. How will I talk to her? I can't move my lips anymore. My eyes just stare out blankly across the room and my hands shake too much to write or signal. How will I let her know I am no longer in the bed but have moved on and am waiting for her in the park beyond?" "It will take time", the spirit says. "If you persist carefully she will come to understand."

And so I begin, knowing this is no small task but a matter of getting ready to communicate my only truly important poems, the ones that last beyond me. I will have to unlearn every cleverness, every borrowed technique, turn of phrase, allusion I've ever picked up. At this point it won't help to know Greek or Latin or Spanish, Chinese or German. Experiences of the world, imaginary locations, fictive personas all useless. I am here in Sydney alone, a rickety hospital with moss-covered sandstone slabs and green-painted drains at the Hyde Park end of Macquarie Street. Maybe I can stretch my consciousness as far as Circular Quay or the steps leading up to the Harbour Bridge. I have three days only to articulate these poems — unlike other poems, they are uniquely for my familiar guardian the enveloping air that, knowing me for so long, will recognize and accept them and for a handful of close loved ones whether living or dead.

This time, moving forward onto the bridge over Macquarie Street, I see the poet from Sydney University I always admired and envied, gone fifteen years ahead of me. I confess to him how much I have learnt from him, how little my own poems seem worth compared to his. He stops me saying, "I learnt a lot from you. It's obvious in my last book which I'll give you now — I could show you the passages that could only be written after reading you — but let me sign a copy for you first." And at that he stepped aside, a few steps off the raised sandstone walkway that suddenly I remember should be called an aula, and hovering there he balanced in mid air, the only place he could comfortably write now, he told me.

The Banker Who Owns the Stars

The banker who owns the stars took me to his observatory on a hill outside Rome. "Look," he said, "that one is where I will live and that one is for my daughter and that one where my wife will live." "Do people who have no money also go to stars after they die?" I ask. "Of course", he shrugs calmly, "they will have to spend their time with the worms but nothing stops a federation of them owning a share in a star. The worms too have their shimmering presence laced in the stillness above and, besides, who can say how many emperors' stars have followed the laws of combustion, dwindling away in the cavalcade of what we can only call the wounds in brightness." "Will the sky and the stars end?" I ask him. He is silent and pulls from his pocket a heavy golden watch within which can be seen smaller golden watches each containing more watches and the last, the smallest, specks of gold sand. The banker is a sober citizen who regulates the profit and loss of the journey. His immense computations are held in a wooden drawer where wands of mercury assess their truth. Now on his outstretched hand specks of brightness are multiplying and I no longer know what is the sky, what the hand, what the unstated sanctuary of luminous decomposing soil.

Shaping the Ideograms

The ideogram for this particular moment is just being shaped. It will join all the other symbols of this earth to signify the conjunction of air, light, wind, moisture and heat that have gathered into this never-to-be-repeated second. No one will fail to recognize this sign the scribe's hand is daubing even now on fragrant yellow paper. Only observe more slowly: watch at a time scale where each hair on the scribe's brush quivers, then comes to rest. All around us, radiance of green, blue, gold and red, streams in unnamable subtleties. The fires of the earth have ended and begun. When all the ideograms are gone, who will appear seated at this table to drink in the breath of now?

The Sea and the Crab's Memory

You have found a way to write about me using only words that hold all things up to be gazed at from the outside. Words that belong in travel documents and phone books, in government legislation, flight protocols, codices for the handling of rare plants or service manuals for the elimination of the past. This is how it has to be, I understand. Narratives of the transforming self have had their day. Intentions and inwardness flicker out like a box of wires and a sputtering headlamp left out in the night rain. It is the brutal age of the limited exhibit – pinned, classified and left to deal with it. The sea has been erased from the crab's memory. For now shells and fossils still speak. Vast creatures have moved through me and scamper into other trees.

The Guardian Angel

I think of madmen with their panpipes circling round you, tilting their misshapen heads into your face. When their hands gesture at decapitation and a pair of them burst out giggling you worry about this experiment in embedding yourself in the modern world. You should have picked some other planet but a lingering addiction to oxygen sucked you in. Your previous visit as a late eighteenth century whale should have warned you off. But as the angel of the depths and the heights you keep returning to us, keep gazing into the eyes of those who suffer and love, keep offering yourself to the fire of our rage.

IV

In The Sleep Of The Riverbed

In the Sleep of the Riverbed

(The riverbed that marks the edge of the mountains adds an extra curve to its journey to converse with the ghost of Federico García Lorca)

1.

Poplars all the way to the sky
and a waterwheel turning
where oranges stencil their perfume
onto the night.

From my passing
I watch the one who does not pass.

The earth grieves
and the eyes of the ox
intent on his harvest of clay.
Grief travels with no footprints
on the dark soil.
The children asleep
in their moist bed under the lemon tree.

Only the mountains don't grieve
and the fiery eyes of the sky.
Ants that will inherit the earth
crave honey the same
as the purple stems
that are the walking coffins of iris.
The water that rushes above me
doesn't grieve
or the vast mirror I ferry helpless

beyond the autumn sun.

From my passing
I watch the one who does not pass.

On the shallow hill
where a lone willow breathes coolness,
who is this man,
companion of eagle and turtle,
diffidently inspecting his shoes
and the tribute of echoes of snow, of wild mint
that come to converse with
his final silence?
Who is this man so filled with life
he has lost speech?

In the deep well where the choirboy drowned
the bull's green eyes
pierce two holes for the wasps to pass.
On the goatgirl's breasts
fragrance of olives and salt cheese.
In the flatlands
the canal of the English
paces a frontier
between death and death.

From my passing
I watch the one who does not pass.

2.

The mountains move always beside me
casting their steady gaze
into the ripples that stream towards sunset.
There, among barren peaks,
birds construct their other world at a crowded pace
with interminable treaties
and sudden revolutions,
negotiating colours forever unknown,

as what vanishes passes over
the small pebbles of the world.

3.

Canals of blood under the skin of the world,
sluggish rivers where microbes
cast their fishing lines of fate.
Paths in the dusty outlands
skirt dry lakes stained with the moon's shadow.
Forests of cypress and poplars gone wild
hiding the magical lizard of fire
and the white deer with blue eyes
who understands the middle name of forgetting.

The king hunts the caged child
alive in the brain's pineal zoo.
The snow-leopard hunts
the small creatures of night
that whisper the secret spell for coolness
when dwelling with death's second cousin,
the sun.

And the flea shelters in the mouth of a wasp
the wasp in the honeyed knuckles of a rock
the rock in the frayed hands of the grass
the grass in the forest

while the immense lost forest of dreaming
shelters in night
and night carves out its shelter
in the still undiscovered voice
locked in the kernel of an almond.

And outside, in all places,
pain awakes,
pain stretches its limbs and awakes in an ant,
in a cricket, in the drop of water
that has inched all night
above the cave where a child bleeds out
the brittle spine of his lungs.

Pain begins its heavy surgical intervention
in the diseased bark of a sapling,
in the tortured frame of a cypress
compulsively vomiting green oxygen.
Pain continues its journey
as the fish hook snagged in the eye of the penis,
as the speck of blue and crimson glass
travelling the infinite hour
between night and dawn.
Pain inscribes its trajectory from
the roots of the oldest elm
to the bud of the opening flower
releasing its prayer to the sky.

4.

(Canticle of the eagle's home)

Little children of stone,
come climb through the back of the mountain.

> Under the sundial of the staid
> potatoes and watercress.
> In the unmeasured sun of the open
> cascades of grapes
> pour their sherries, their muscats and ports
> for the far colony of the English.
> How much torn-up earth
> to feed a vanishing world.

Little children of stone,
come climb through the back of the mountain.

Through the back of the mountain
enter the head of a vulture
or the perpetual snow
lodged in the eyes of an eagle.
Sleep is there
when we find it speaking our name.

Little children of stone,
the plotted world of canals,
of the spider's abacus,
is no homeland.

5.

It wasn't easy, gathering thin veins of will,
sending them up through rock and hard clay
to produce this raw shadow of a ghost.
How much easier it would have been
to stay flat in the grave's anonymity,
to be no one nestled in nowhere.

What *is* it being human?

Suddenly overtaken
by the great forest of the dead,
my arms fall useless, my body closes
as if everything inside it
had been taken out:
bowels and liver,
spleen and muscles
but also names, futures,
the whole interwoven caul
of tomorrows and yesterdays —
the fine-tuned knife of the world
in one slow moment
doing its job inside me.

What happened
isn't true.
I had not died.

6.

Who sews the cloaks for those small grey birds
that pass invisibly between snow and fire?
Under whose direction do the dreams of the mountains
follow this fluid curve that rushes
towards its own vanishing?
Who pronounces the name of each leaf
as it feels its colour
draining back into the sky,
the husk of its being
lifted by the wind?

        Across the exploding eyes
        a horse tramples the long
        fingers of the cemeteries.
        Irises grow through the bones
        of unborn foals
        and the thunderous echo of a river's birth
        can be heard quite clearly by lovers
        a thousand miles deep in the earth.

When the name Hope is erased
in the space where stars were,
who glides around me as I sleep?

        The devastated moon
        reads off its history in the double canal
        where summer and winter stand equal guard
        over the childhood of water.
        Squirrels patrol the upper reaches of the earthly tree.
        Softly, with no knowledge of grief's pre-history,
        a fly in its canoe

made from the waxed dust of asteroids
rows patiently across the lake
of the inner ear.
In the womb
listening is everything.

7.

(*Kyrie of the riverbank spider*)

Suspended in threads of light,
why does a cold black honey
seep into the ascetic's prayer of waiting?
Scattered like a story drained of time
bits of everywhere dazzle in green oblivion,
mirrored in this river
that has forgotten how to flow.

To awaken
clenched in the embrace of no one.
To be the lover of an empty sighing
drifting to me as the wind
fades out.

Across the river's stillness
a thunderstorm is building
the brusque first syllables of language.
All my life
my entrails were slowly giving birth
to death.

8.

The clouds lie under the water
and the faces of mountains
and very old elms
that have understood dreaming,
how it is
to awake as another.

Beautiful body of the lover,
only for you do I take off my watch,
only for you do I take off time
and enter the pool of your eyes,
becoming this kiss
that awakes me,
gliding under the skin of the world.

Night and sunrise
step equally through me.
Here on this low rise,
among crumbling leaves,
accepting today and yesterday equally.

Bubbles break from the holed boat
in its race to find the mud.
Petals folded around
the heavy bodies of flies
spin against the abolished clock
and the carcass of a crow
spins one last time
before going under.
Only the constellation of longing still
floats in my embrace.

The roots of the willow
pass over and through me.
Embraced by the ant and the star,
now I have finally shed time,
the unnecessary foliage
stained with the fragrance of loss.

Under the water
lie clouds, the faces of mountains
and the battered half-coin of the moon
that understands
how to be what it dreams.

9.

Epilogue: the unheard voices.

(fern on the canal's bank)

Though fear soars
over and around me
my weight is a single
green word.

(waterwheel)

Turning and turning
to the slow drip of the sky,
I bring life to the orange grove,
to the sugar beet basking in sunlight.
With no concern for wind or faltering starlight

I lift and measure abundance
watching the receding fields shine back.
Lifting and letting go,
my trembling hands
fill and empty.

(the course of the river)

I who have been the wavering frontier
between fertile land and the realm of mountain and snowfall,
a relaxed swimmer, spinning and gliding
past busy inland wharves where dreams are traded,
tugged by the slow mud
that drifts across marshlands,
at last spreading out to trace
the intricate pubic triangle of the delta,
I find in all that meanders towards its birth
the weight of my own being.

(turtle)

Beloved face
tilted towards finding
with all the quiet depth of the river
welling up in the grey
awakening of eyes –

it is not only the dint of your
familiar shell
moulded into the shadow

of this long branch —
not only how your neck
twists to acknowledge
my clumsy feet edging me down
into the half-lit world of minnows
and tiny bugs.

When you love someone
their ancestors for a hundred generations
become your ancestors,
their offspring
for a hundred generations your offspring,
our touch rippling out
to the still white blessing
of stars.

Selected Poems:
1988 – 2009

From Instructions Given to the Royal Examiners in the State of Chi

Examine the candidate's state of mind
as he inscribed the answers to all of the above
and estimate the temperature of his brain cells
as he lay awake in the cubicle at night
longing for the raw oysters with calamansi juice of home.
Assess the longevity of his nails
as they quivered lightly over the brushstrokes,
the density of his gaze as he reread the instructions.
Reckon to the nearest decimal place
the honesty of his bones
as he let memory drain into the page.
Calculate according to established formula
the expression of his face, old or young,
as his lips guessed the first hushed sounds of the rhythm
and fix clearly in your mind what lay behind that face,
the trembling moment of pure emptiness.
Identify the direction of the wind
as it hurries the leaves of all the provinces
away from everything known,
brushing them with the fragrance
of unnamed creatures waiting to be born.
Remember for what purpose
you are setting down these dreams
under such limited starlight.
Remember the waves which are forcing you
further and further off all courses into the terrible wilderness of death.
Then forget all of yourself and all your hopes
and write your mark and comments in the correct space
for the perusal of a higher order.

Separation

You in the high-walled fortress of sleep
I on an island of wakefulness
bird-haunted, trapped by mist

You eyeing the warm milk of suspicion
I drinking the green rain of the seagull's ocean

You on the red deck of the last ferry going under
I on the amusement pier lost in the crowd

You going forward into the mirror
I crawling backward into the teeth's cavity

You in sunglasses
walking towards the sea on a street that backs into the sun
I sliding on ice across the abandoned freeway

You in prison waiting for redemption
I in the asylum counting billiard balls

You climbing stairways, humping buckets of soapy fisheyes
I descending the silver elevators, escorted by clouds

You on the night bus that leaves from the ferry wharf and goes
across the stone desert to the other side of the earth
I on the top floor of the brightly lit hospital,
beating the glass with my hands

The night is cold
The poplars are grey in the headlights

You have opened the paragraph of silence
I was closing the volume of inaudible sound

Midwinter Swimming

I dream of the pool which is still open,
its long lanes under floodlight.
At the counter
a sultry gymnast
rolls langourous coins for the turnstile.
Before me
the vast overheated hall's
lit up like a spaceship
afloat in subtropical night,
and everywhere
sparse shapes are poised for demolishing distances.
Rows of orange markers
sway in the wake of lumbering middle-aged tigers
or matrons with varicosed thighs
white and blue as the Argentine flag;
while on the starter's block,
lean and rapt,
like St Sebastian in a swoon of arrows,
the body poised
as for the opening of the future.

Moving House

Rows of icons grace the small house behind the monastery.
Nestling beside the railway line
it lacks a kitchen but the sunroom has a stove.
In the square-shaped lounge room
weddings and children multiply
in photographs the size of Chinese woks
nailed to the rafters.
This is a house built for close perusal by giants.
The insignia of the lawn lead to a study built next to
a tumbledown garage.
In the front garden the owner occupier
is feeding tea leaves to a favourite rosebush.
The creases of his hands give nothing away
though tomorrow they will seem foreign
like the snow in a postcard
like the grin left on a pillow
when you sleepwalk through the wall.

At the threshold of the house
two bedrooms greet you
with the discreet fulfilment of needs
hushed in thick carpet.
The family has fled to the old country.
Only the father remains to complete the transaction,
his scorched gardener's face
muffled by a blue handkerchief.
At this price
you would be crazy not to buy.

Four Variations on a Text of St John

1

I stopped at the well.
The busload of tourists with whom I travelled
had gone ahead into the village
to trade their dollars
for bananas chapatis couscous crabs and red cheese.
Pariah women with bracelets of gold
watched from the door of a broken hut
by a pile of smoking garbage.
I had no living water to offer
only shekels airfares walkmen third world debt
and one night immunity,
while outside all night
the wind of desolation
roared.

2

I stopped at the well,
the sun still blazing in deserted sky.
They led me down lanes from the marketplace
to a backalley cricket bat factory
opposite a door of sunlight
where a boy sat limp on a paliset
with twisted paralysed legs.
We looked a little at each other.
I felt within me
no power, no force,
only a double paralysis.

Beyond the silence
the world was rushing
in planes aircon buses jeepneys nuclear rockets.
I did not ask for water.
I did not offer water.
In one village I drank chai,
in another Coca Cola.

3

The wide hills were green and tall with barley
and they rippled across his mind.
At that moment
fish were listening.
At that moment
gunships were poised over distant villages.
At that moment
the world was formed complete.
On a stone within the well's shadow
watching this woman bending and lifting
the heavy bucket of water.
She had entered heaven five times
and he was to be the sixth
so he unstrapped the tetracycline from the inside of his thigh
and the woman stepped
within the ambience of truth.
Perhaps the veil covered her completely
so he could only guess
at her face her age.
Her hand from under the black cloth
reached forward
like the coarse knuckles of death
and he recited his litany:

I come from beyond the blackout.
I have crossed the river of darkness
strapped to a burnt out raft

and she exchanged
after all
not breast or cunt
but a ladle of tepid black water
while he waited
caught out for once and shamed
as she lay down at the feet
of this slender god of the future.

4

I stopped at the well and I asked for water.
It was late on a hot day.
Shapes in drab cloaks sidled away
like smoke in the dusty heat-haze of the plain.
Like an old ship battered by storms
that creeps into the shining harbour,
unwelcome,
unannounced:
whatever I gave was
as one gives crushed strawberries
heavy with too much sweetness.

So I carried off my guilt
dragging these limbs across centuries
to rest
beside the glib shine of omiyage dolls
in a hut by the inland sea

where I watch the bay descend in broken lines.
By night
a ferryboat shuffles the curve of sleek waters.

The West's sagas run out.
Broken swirls of blue ink
on the sign over a noodle shop;
shrapnel and soft drink, souvenirs of hands;
a river ending in lacquered gold.

When Eagles Pause to Talk with Your Sleeping Body

When you wake again
the donkey will be standing idly in the road,
the old man will open his shop,
the seagulls will tread critically
among the piles of garbage,
wind will flap small religious photographs
pegged to the ice cream stall,
the old woman and her daughter
will be sitting under the black cross
near the santo ninyo,
a man from the desert will go mad
in the bar by the marketplace,
a boy bandaged like a doll
will gaze from the tenth story window.

When you wake again
dusk will be falling across the harbour,
fishing boats will be rocking by the stone wharf,
cold night air will ripple the line of water,
a sinker will fall from a bridge
and bury itself in darkness,
the last train will climb the hill
turning its back on the sea.

When you wake again
drunks will skate in wide circles over the pond,
the ice cream seller will fold up his van,
a blonde-haired stranger will stroll uphill
with melons and cheese for dinner,

the neon signs will come on
and tomorrow's clothes will hang in unopened wardrobes.

When you wake again
a favourite pillow will cover a magic toy car
that glows all night in the wind of silence,
a voice will cry out in a dream,
a woman will open the door
and recognise only the layer of dust on your shoes.

When you wake again
your life will fill the house
like a tap left running day and night
for a thousand years.

When you wake again
when the balcony crumbles at last
into the swimming pool
when eagles pause to talk with your sleeping body.

Robert Frost at Eighty

I think there are poems greater and stranger than any I have known.
I would like to find them.
They are not on the greying paper of old books
or chanted on obscure lips.
They are not in the language of mermaids
or the sharp-tongued adjectives of vanishing.
They run like torn threads along paving stones.
They are cracked as the skull of an old man.
They stir in the mirror
at fifty,
at eighty.
My ear keeps trying to hear them
but the seafront is cold.
The tide moves in.
They migrate like crows at a cricket ground.
They knock at the door when I am out.

I have done with craft.
How can I front ghosts with cleverness,
the slick glide of paradox and rhyme
that transforms prejudice
to brittle gems of seeming wisdom?

Though I bury all I own or hold close
though my skin outlives the trees
though the lines fall shattering the stone
I cannot catch them.
They have the lilting accent
of a house I saw but never entered.
They are the sounds a child hears —

the water, the afternoon, the sky.
I watch them now
trickling through the open mirror.
Sometimes, but almost never,
we touch what we desire.

The Joys of Mathematics

At fifty I will begin my count towards the infinite numbers.

At negative ninety-nine I will start my walk towards the
    infinitessimally small.

At one over twenty-seven I will inspect the first bridgeworks.

At twenty two over seven I will write a message in a bottle, entrust it to
    a sea turtle, slip under a wave and sleep.

At eighty-seven sparrows will land on the windowsill, pecking a hole
    that leads inside my arm.

At 127 I will begin to arrange the children's pillows, carefully filling
    each one with warm handfuls of snow.

At ten to the negative six our friends from the White House will arrive,
    handing out glass beads and broken shells filled with recently
    perfected poisons.

At the inverse square of sixteen the sky will curve over blue
    lakes, songbirds settle at dusk, a small train rattle off
    towards a village that leans against a single church spire.

At one over negative twenty-two I will start to dream in Sanskrit,
    creating a swarm of brown ants to bring back
    a baby's rattle from the edge of a mud slide.

At ten to negative two over three I will open my heart, letting go of all
    vanities, right down to the wilted bones.

At the third transfinite number I will give up easy answers.

At e to the i pi the earth will bristle with skulls and weapons, dolphins
   will proclaim the first inter-stellar arms bazaar in Antarctica,
   the new born will drink only lead, the elderly will wander the
   moon in the quest for warmth.

At one I will open my eyes.

At zero I will put the key back under the mat.

Kinderszenen

1

You are my friend.
You talk to me out of grey sky and thin soup.
You penetrate my wrist with love words.
You grate my toes like wheat
to scatter my loneliness among birds.
You wear my eyes
so I will glow in darkness.

In the double ward
laughter is crying.
The train on the wall
stretches from March to October.
Thirteen, the cars he draws
look like striped sausage dogs.
Sugar, stained pink,
travels through his throat into his eyes
and rises
as a blue cloud of crying.

2

Nine years old, maybe seven,
she had a hole in her head the size of a thumb.
She walked the hospital's open veranda
in her stained dressing gown,
her face tilted like a skinned hatchet,
all the dark constellations above her
draining into two blank eyes.

Faces like the plucked pears of childhood –
wizened prune eyes –
my double in the child's pain ward,
she glitters now in night sky,
ghost glowing
that burns the fingertips of daylight.

3

Three a.m.
You lie head tucked down,
flattened like a turtle.
Your tiny hands curl downward
into sleep and dreams,
scooping fistfuls of wet eddying warmth
while the mouth works constantly
as if transforming this alien flood
to the soft purring babble of voice.
        From the hallway I watch you,
little elf king of coldness stretched out again, wrestling
        out of blankets
into a night sky of brittle years.
Contorting your limbs
you swim against the rush of elements
while the earth tilts against me.

The Colours of Ageing

(*Anacita's poem*)

The avocados in autumn age under black skins,
their green smell like mossy stones under a waterfall.
In the kitchen reach out and touch
the smooth slime.
In my country we eat them with ice-cream
or tinned sweetened milk.
My father in his workday singlet
would leave his portion for me
and go out
to be alone with the chooks.
In the floral nightdress she wore all day
till the sun bleached the red from the roses
my mother is fussing and flailing.
Afraid of her hard hand
we rush out, my brothers and me,
to hide under the palm trees as the first rains come down.

All that was long ago.
The trees grow now in a different autumn.
Seen through winter frost a lone palm
rises out of excavated earth.
Derelict walls turn their backs on the sun
and I age under this skin of woven cloth.
The cicadas along the riverbank find nothing
except the black sleeves of their discarded livery.
Their shrill moan
traces in evening air
all that was green.

On Sydney's South-West Line

The RSL club fakes nightlife
with its few gaudy lights.
Beside the line
rows of red brick flats where
darkened cars slumber.
Stations at the end of the long journey
from Saigon or Bucharest or El Salvador.

I come from a country
where civilisation only exists
in cities and in tall buildings.
One day the small boys took over
and shot those over twenty-five,
then the tribes rallied
hoping to fall on the capital,
then the Russians arrived,
then the Americans poured money and weapons
into the hands of bandits
and the cities shook under rocket attacks
and the night sky blazed like a festival,
then the tribes clapped their hands
and everyone who could
left.

Smells in cupboards unleashing the past:
a rainy Sunday
couples coming out of the underground,
young man in military uniform
the girl distracted playing with his hand
kissing him as if he had already gone.

The woman turns the photos to the wall
she says it is unlucky to reveal someone's photo
tempting fate with images.

Arriving in Australia 6.30 a.m.
the city streets empty and quiet
as though we had come home from the world.

"The people say she not live anymore"
The translation happens somewhere in the heart
when the mind has given up on the battle.

What could we do
our lives scattered like dice on the table
only to work all year
to pay off the cost of the airfare
the cost of the finder
the expense of the interest on the cost
in barbed wire barracks
on the desert's white fringe.

Sydenham Station 6 a.m.
on the overhead bridge
in the damp chill of early morning
the crowd all migrants mostly women
rushing from platform to platform
having got up having eaten at five
mucho trabajo y poco dinero.

In five minutes the body is taken away
the injured are taken away
someone will clean the blood off the streets
and everything will be normal.

If you buy food for your family
in five days your month's salary is gone.
I don't think the fighting will ever stop
because there is no *hadaf* no *but* :
each group fighting, killing with no *hadaf* no *but* –
no aim or reason –
and the women and children
living in fear
living on death
living on the money from drugs
drugs for the world:
heroine and cocaine:
to fund the armies
to feed the children.

What to make of what happens
when people survive the eye of Auschwitz or Pol Pot
and settle down at the world's last doorstep
what to make of this land
where the only art that's alive
is electronic noise blasting the walls of pubs
where a poet finds South America
at the bottom of the tenth bottle of Actifed CC
that saddest of drugs.

I was five years old when my father was sent to the re-education camp.
My mother had to go out all day to work and I was left alone in the
house. I sat very frightened on the floor. I didn't want people to see me.
The neighbours kept away from us because of their fear after what
happened to my father. After a few years I didn't want to talk anymore.

A river is strapped to my shoulders –
all its weight is there

every time I stretch out my hand
to turn the key in a door.

Below the line of trees
the bay lies sleek and restless.
Long outrigger canoes
jostle the shoreline –
here where the road dies
among coconut palms and thatched huts
a day like any other
for the americanos to order beer and crabs.
When the mountain shook the first time
my sister was in the change room.
You have to realise how proud we all were
when she got the job as receptionist
because a job after all
especially when you don't have relatives in the government.
She felt nervous, under pressure –
she had to be so careful
with her co-workers waiting to catch her out
so she used to go into the change room a lot
because she could eat her food there
without being seen
and that's where she was
two days later
when they dug her out –
she was the only one to survive
because the air could reach her there
down a long tunnel.

The sun lies flat on the river:
whitewashed houses grip tightly about themselves.
Bluish grass grows down to the water;

drowsy heads of thistles dry in the heat.
Fear enters
from the giant screen
from the tiniest insect:
almost with the first words it came
blocking you from the things the words named.
My little boy calls the bats he sees on television "butterflies".
Instinctively he fears them –
these sharp-edged black butterflies
fluttering in darkness.

We were waiting in a queue in the Palace of Communications
when all the lights went out –
a series of bombs could be heard
like little mushrooms
dropped on the floor of darkness
all over the city.
We said to each other:
it is really happening:
and we stood quite still
wondering what would be left.

Evening sky over Hue:
a couple in flame-coloured clothes
walking at sunset among tall trees,
quiet words in the ancestral garden,
the gentle pressure of hand on hand.

I didn't find you in the beachfront restaurant –
only your emptied bowl in the back kitchen.
I was racing towards a department store
hoping to see you in the mirrors.
At the central telephone exchange

the operator connected me with the wrong continent
then interrupted my dialling and said
"The people say she not live anymore."

The woman turns the photos to the wall.

The small cries of love
that night in a paper-thin bungalow
under mosquito netting
the sounds of love from the room next door
the altered breathing the sighs
so brief and then silence
and moving over both of us
a force tugging at the waist
so that on the floor surrounded by sisters and brothers
nieces and aunties
in that narrow room of the barrio
the same dream settled on both of us
like a blockage of the throat and of the heart
and we woke and faced each other
our hands had become artisans of death
our lips beakers of abundant water
daylight was cries of chickens
the whine of a water pump
listening in the long hour before dawn
to the endless crying of a child
somewhere out in the darkness.

Outside Redfern station: 4.30 p.m.
the express is stalled in a wilderness of lines.
From the crowded carriage
the skyline of the city is brown with smog.
Each face lifts

towards an enormous clock
its black arms stuck in time.

In the metal scoop they are washing in brisk water
and what they don't want
is shaken off
and falls past my window.
They speak sparingly
and seem unhurried:
two grey birds
for whom my roof is home.

Education

Seven years old,
on loan to an uncle
and a bundle of cash went missing.
For three days locked in a room, beaten.
The golden orbs of pennies roasted in an oven
removed by tongs
glisten on a child's skin
as she screams and screams.
These round white scars
that remain even today
without pigment
without the shadow of colour
with only the ash's afterglow.

After telling that story
you burnt your hand on the iron,
burnt it yourself,
your punishment for breaking silence.

You rushed to the balcony but they pulled you back inside.
You wanted to spit, to scream insults at the soldiers
to stop them beating up the old man in the street.
"Listen," she said as she held you back, your mother.
"Listen, you have to learn to say nothing."
Learn to be nobody.
Learn to be the white wall
that has no face and no tongue.

November in Madrid

At the Florida Bar on Gran Via an agent for fame asks how long I have been in the country. He pays for the drink. A brandy never tasted so much like a fiery emptiness.

In a place where, wanting so intently, I burn and cannot imagine how that fire did not convert the world.

This tumbler of raw alcohol without ice has been waiting a lifetime to offer me this street, this fall of light, this sensation of walking on water along a common pavement, uncertain of the depths that open before the smallest step.

Opposite a small square formed by a twist in the road so like the bus stop where twenty years before I fled, an abrupt adolescent terrified of closeness.

An older man whom I respected and loved once said, "You are pushing away someone who holds you in her heart above all things. You may not know it now, but one day you will and there is no pain as sharp as regret." That time has come. That time has been here a long time.

At the Florida Bar on Gran Via I step out to catch a last taxi in the drizzle of early morning.

By trying to be someone different I have turned into myself.

Homage to Federico Mompou

Federico Mompou (1893- 1987), a Catalan composer, created numerous delicate miniatures for the piano.

The holy city should have a name so small
there is almost none of it left to grace a grave with.
It should be a trail of lost breath in the air
or a hand
left dangling on the walk to
the Museum of Spare Parts.
Small birds hover round it
or chirp at its mirage
from dusty grass by the roadside.
It should have the shape
of an ornate overbrimming fountain
buried somewhere
near a subway station nobody uses.

Even though
even though
the weight of August lies on the land
and a small man with a ludicrous hat
poses for a photograph beside the winged angel
in a grey park opposite the glare of the traffic;
even though at sunset you walk unscathed
through the obvious air
with an unbearable weight on your shoulders
the dead are there on both sides of the river
you let go now of their bright chatter
drifting in a boat with the last of the tide
fashioner of silent music.

Owl Song

White shadows poured on the black sky:
owls with a longing for
the impermanence of zebras.

*

It rests above my shoulder
like a knife in cold water:
the owl mask
draped in a passionfruit vine.

*

A singular burn at the core of the hand:
the owl's eyes in midsummer.

*

They have gone down the avenue ahead of me
and rest in a mirror of ice.

*

A woman without ears
is transported
across the desert
by ravens:
owls cowering by a pool
darkened with blood.

*

A highway lifts off the map
and ripples gently
between two beckoning stars:
owls remaking their corridor of earth.

*

Droning escapes my throat
and lodges in monumental concrete:
the sound of owls
descends to the bottom of a lake
some years after extinction.

*

I met an owl once
on the threshold of childhood –
a silver shadow
between myself and the laundry.

*

White feathers,
the tight clenching of a grey
claw-like
face.

*

Radiant zithers leave the mountainside at dawn:
they are the dream thoughts of owls.

*

Raw shakuhachi drone in the icy tavern:
an owl
leaving the world.

César Vallejo

Dead these sixty years in Paris
where rain and snow once more
bury the hungry boulevards,
you stand head bowed
above what seems to be a gravestone,
the wide hat of a ranchero in your hand
and with the grimace of a man who loses all in a cockfight.
Amigo,
I hear the shrill song that flows under your breath.
In darkest nightmare summoning the names of all colours
you mutter so quietly
the savage diction of a cerebral chemist.

Or I meet you in the hospital
where polishers whirr
enormous circles on the moonlit floor.
The X-rays tacked up on the wall,
their dark scrawl
threading the pain of the earth to the pain of the stars.
A white bird drops by saying "Open this door."
The curtain of your sickbed waits to move
like the sail of a ship.
In Peru the horse of your childhood
still chews its grass, tosses its mane
in the last dryness of summer.
A poem or a life
ripples between such trivial and such portentous matter,
incorporates derision,
dispenses its own handshakes.

And if after so many words
not one word.
And if among so many breaths
not one sigh
crosses the vacuum.

In a dream you woke to find the windowsill opposite your bed
lined with money,
little gold and silver coins that shone at you.
In the next room the same
and at the front door
a row of coins the same.

Such embarrassing gifts among bandaged heads.
Bloom of putrefaction on the skin
of the one who guards twilight.
Graced always with the wealth of the air,
César Vallejo,
under Paris rain
seeking the correct and final gesture,
giving these aesthetic otherworldly objects
their human name.

Lament for Ignacio Sanchez Mejías.

(after the Spanish of Federico García Lorca)

1. Goring and death

a las cinco de la tarde
at five in the afternoon
a boy brought the white sheet
a las cinco de la tarde
wind scattered balls of cottonwool
a las cinco de la tarde
the dove in the leopard's claws
a las cinco de la tarde
base notes in the drum's belly
a las cinco de la tarde
a thigh and a desolate horn
a las cinco de la tarde
smoke and arsenic in the ring of church bells
a las cinco de la tarde
the snow was dripping sweat
and iodine covered the bullring
the rest was death and only death
a las cinco de la tarde.

For his bed they wheel in a coffin.
Dry bones and recorders jar the ears.
Rainbows of pain on the hospital wall.
Gangrene sets in, like an old tramp taking off dusty shoes beside a bed.
The crowd at the window beating their fists on the glass.
a las cinco de la tarde.
a las cinco de la tarde.
Five by all the clocks

five in the afternoon
five in the long shadow of the afternoon.

2. Spilt Blood.

Que no quiero verla.
I don't want to see it.

Tell the moon to rise early
for I don't want to see
Ignacio's blood on the sand.
The moon,
horse of frozen clouds
in the grey arena of dreams
where willow trees graze beyond barriers,
I don't want to see it.

Memory burns.
The jasmine trees flutter white handkerchiefs.
The cow of the old world
rolls its sad tongue along a snout
laced with blood.
The bulls of Guisando
half death half stone
groan like two hundred years
of crunching the stiff earth.
Ignacio's body moves up the grandstand,
the weight of death crushing his shoulders.
In the quest for his perfect shadow
he looked for dawn
and there was no dawn.
He looked for the beauty of his body

and met his own blood emptied in a long spurt
like the flair of streamers.
I don't want to see it –
that moment of translucent agony
splashed against the jeans and leather of a crowd on heat.
Who shouts to have a look?
Don't tell me to look.

His eyes were open
when the horns bore in.
The terrible mothers, the Dark Ones,
tilted his head into death.
No prince in Seville was his match –
gladiator of this Andalusian Rome,
mountaineer gentle among wheat,
shining star of the fiesta crowd
lightly holding the spiked barbs.
Late afternoon light
trembled caressing his head.

Now there is only sleep.
Dry grass picks the flower of his skull.
His blood sings across
lonely swamps and high green pastures,
beyond the bulls' horns stiff with cold,
lost with a thousand hoof-beats,
this nightingale of severed veins
like a long dark tongue of sadness
dumped in the starry Guadalquivir.
I don't want to see it.

No chalice holds that blood.
No swallows gulp it down.

No white frost of first light chills it.
Lilies in an avalanche can't make it white.
No mirror can coat it in the miracle of silver.
No,
I don't want to see it.

3. In the body's presence

La piedra es una frente donde los sueños gimen
sin tener agua curva ni cipreses helados.
This stone slab is a young man's forehead where the dreams
keep spinning
and never reach the ocean
or the cold branches of the cypress trees.
The stone pavement is time's heavy shoulder,
its tree trunk of tears, trophies and planets.

I once saw grey rain lash the sea
lifting tender pockmarked arms
to escape the delicate stone.

The stone carries seeds and clouds,
diminutive skeletons of skylarks and twilight wolves,
but no echo, no glass, no fire,
only arenas and more arenas and, beyond that, more
arenas of barren stone.

Now Ignacio the brave lies on that stone.
Death has washed his face with sulphur
and placed upon his head the mask of a dark minotaur.

Now it is over. Rain penetrates his mouth.

Wind like a wild animal licks his chest.
His sex saturated with tears of snow
craves the warmth of a haystack's shadow.

What is said isn't the truth.
We stand and watch a corpse collapse,
the clear silhouette of a nightingale
decomposing into a handful of syringes.

I want to see here the men with hard voices,
those who master horses and own rivers,
who dream of clean picked bones and sing, their mouths full of the sun
and cobbled lanes that lead to quiet harbours.

I want to see them here. Before the stone pavement.
Before this corpse of broken reins.
I want them to tell me where is the exit
for this captain tethered to death.

I want them to teach me a lament like a river
of soft clouds and deep shores
to lift Ignacio's body and lose it
without hearing the redoubled breathing of the bull,

that his body disappear in the moon's round arena,
on a songless night of fishes
in the white pus of frozen smoke.

Don't cover his face with a handkerchief.
Don't make him grow used to death.
Look, Ignacio: don't you feel the hot roar of the bull.
Sleep, rest: the sea also dies.

4. Life vanished.

The bull doesn't know you nor the fig tree
nor horses nor the ants that swarmed across your house.
The afternoon doesn't know you nor the small boy in the doorway
now you have died forever.

The stone's spine doesn't know you
nor the black landscape of your death.
Your own memory doesn't know you
now you have died forever.

Autumn will return with snails,
grapes dusted with snow and broad shouldered mountains lying at rest,
but no one will stop to gaze into your eyes
now you have died forever.

Now you have died forever
like all the dead of the earth
like all who lie forgotten
in the mountain of snuffed dogs.

No one knows you. But still I sing of you,
your shadow and grace.
It will be a long time till there is born
an Andalusian so clear, so rich in living.
I sing your elegance in keening words
and recall a sad breeze among the olive groves.

First Shift

The clothes of the absent woman
who is cold and heavy with sleep
rest easy by night in the darkened kitchen.
Numb with tiredness she will stumble and fix their floral delicacy
to her neck and breasts
and the loveless day will drag against her eyes.
Over and over she will find
the sink where her teeth are waiting,
find the chill of the open window
where the steam of the kettle escapes.
And the single cup of coffee
will be bitter and strong
under the small light she turns on cautiously
so as not to disturb the children
who must wake later on
and dress themselves
and eat the breakfast she leaves out
in the bowls she arranges.

The clothes hang from the back of the fridge
to warm themselves.
All night they stay awake,
the consciousness of a house without a voice.
Later she will watch the steam rise
against her fingers as she drinks,
will quickly carefully check the latch when leaving.
Walking rapidly through the darkness
towards the first train
she won't even think of endings or purposes.

The earth's cold has many names.
To walk and to breathe
will have to count as living.

Marriage

The fish around us are wide and lonely.
They do not have your eyes.
A single trail of bubbles
lifts your thoughts
towards the bright rim of survival.
Up there
a mouth as beautiful as yours
smears my lips with seaweed.
In the tangled meshing of sleepiness
I could extend my arm
to push us both towards
whatever normality broken surfaces bring.
I'm not sure
if your breath can carry mine
and though I hold you
I always dream of letting go.
I tell myself the light in your window
is not the light of heaven
but the fish have swum into the room
and in this circle of the cosmos
shining voices resonate
in old tins as they drift
downward to the ocean's private doss-house.

Too late to be anywhere else.
My hand and yours are almost the same size.

At Age Sixteen

The steps within our steps
the inner rhythm that walks us.
    I go past the parked cars
past the green edges of adolescence
descending a hill where the sea trails
its weary vein of blue fire.
There are houses with windows open.
There are doors that guard the light they should give out.
Party days.
In an upstairs room
the girls are changing, still preparing themselves
and someone is practising French from records just bought.
Their glances are for the handsome one,
the tall musician with blond hair
who will come here after I am gone.
In the lounge-room a phone purrs inconsolably
where the other side of the earth is waiting
to enter my ear.
    Even back then it would have been the time to cross over
with the wind blowing and the long afternoon unravelling.
Arms draped on balconies
like the shadow of longing.
Wineglasses on windowsills
filled to the brim with sunlight.
No one will ever quite enter the sea.

After Music of Prokofiev

The moon is over the meadows.
Soft-eyed and sad
the cow wanders the lawn.
Quietly devastated by love
a hair carves a semi-circle on the page

The ladder goes down to the pool where you swim,
the grey skull cap peaked about your pixie ears.
White flesh on the operating table,
a bag of intestines strapped to your chest,
silver sheen of the age that walks in your feet.

The music points to the space where the music ends:
the breath is there,
flat and quiet,
moving over the earth's slow plains
toward the mountains.

You have walked down the long colonnade
of a hot European July evening,
the statues as alive
as the trees that lead to the harbour,
and everywhere
at your shoulder
the birds are talking their own languages.

For My Father

The young man carries his child around the garden of the new house, his son encased in iron, the one who will never walk.

The fish are under the surface of the pond. Their backs, encrusted with greenness, ripple in and out as they trace the eye of the watching child.

The father's arms are enormous as he walks. His feet measure the backyard and the sky to the same regular beat.

A gentle rain questions the earth. There is no voice in the eye that dreams. Two years old, they lock him into the narrow room above the garden he can't see in the feverish darkness.

The hospital's narrow room, the corridor backing onto daylight, only you know, not I, father, dying inch by inch these twenty years, stroking up the river of throttled anger.

The flowers by the bedside are dying rapidly now. On the table, in the vase where they suffer, their heads are shrinking and shrinking. No one asked for them. No one speaks for them. These flowers are clenched as tight as swallowed paper, as the dark core of the sun seen from the inside.

We sit down in doorways. We thread our fingers through the skyline. We watch water tumbling out of empty skies.

The son writes the words for the father who no longer reads. The father carries the house of tenderness in which he can no longer place the son.

Boats sail past unconcerned. The wharf reaches out into deeper and deeper water. The wake of liners foams above this place where whales once turned slowly to gaze at receding stars.

There is no danger in the needles which carry death. Their sweet long tips drool in the icetrays all the hot summer twilight. The nurse knows only meticulous floors where moonlight is drawing cartoons of upturned rowboats, vast trawling nets that fix us to the seabed with not a sound glimmering up out of that stillness.

Outside of time stones gathered from the field are placed one on another to form a wall. The young man setting the heavy stones in the wall is the father. The son crosses oceans, boards planes, finds himself at nightfall on dilapidated backroads where dogs howl and the only place to go is a bare room with contaminated water in a jug on the table. The son drinks.

Rain taps at the window demanding to come in. The father is alone in the house where the walls are himself. He wanders stairwells and landings, searching for proverbs and toothpicks. The two sides of his body speak different languages.

We walk oceans to find this. We come gliding over water. We fashion keys out of dust.

The father's hand, grown a stranger, cannot find its way to a tap or a cup.

The child screams in the darkness every night.

Last Things

A single piece of fruit
drains all the light from the room,
becomes black and heavy
saturated with the emptiness that surrounds it.
In the hallway
the children's voices have long gone
and anger flickers somewhere behind my eyes
like a worn socket spluttering in a bulb.
I had always imagined something other than this.
      As the breath grows shallower
as the ear rings in a house of blackness
as the goat path disappears
into cold mist and slippery boulders.
Small things betray us.
The jaw that aches as the oxygen dwindles.
Deep and delicate this depression
as it walks across me into the other world.
At this hour
I am always the one who arrives at the farthest edge,
the dishevelled one who returns,
who has seen rivers flow backwards into the sky.
An eye outside the world looks back.

The fruit of darkness
lies cool and plump in the palm of a girl's slender hand.
She offers me the last portion,
the first fruit.

In the Small Hours

It's three a.m. in the morning
of a day you won't enter for so many hours.
Where you are
yesterday's sunlight still bathes your feet as you walk
and tonight hearing your voice
I worried that one day
I'll lose my images of all those I love.
Outside the city's still restless:
taxis alert and shiny as golden birds
waiting for the crumbs of dawn.
At fifty five I know so little how to live.
In cafes across this city
lovers still hold hands
and cups balance on the edges of tables.
Darkness falls around me like soft snow.
Beside the narrow bed
my night-light is staring right into me.
I will hold your voice inside me as long as I can.
When I sleep you'll go on walking
through a steady explosion of white flowers.

Cecile

No one will phone you up tonight
and I won't smell ever again the *nuoc mam*
and red slivers of uncooked meat,
the fistfuls of flowering coriander
rising in steam from your bowl
as you ate in your room alone.
No more animated small talk
in the gentle fierce abrasion of half French
or tracing your wanderings on the map
or preserving the silent rapture you needed
to watch *"Prisonière"*,
your one hour's weekly self-improvement in Strine.

Of the two of us
I'm the only one to reach the Andes,
that high rim of the world you always travelled towards.
I'll never sort out your stories –
India, Nice, Hanoi, the Isle of Pines –
and I keep expecting to find
somewhere among my papers
your snapshot of two Iranian students
posing shyly under Tehran's wintry trees
while at their back
the cars, exploding, curl into black smoke.

Everything's interwoven now
like the beads you threaded for your jewellery
                        to hawk at the Cross.
The night I first got cancer
I stumbled into the post-op ward with N,

my friend, your lover, to visit you —
your thin being and extraordinary hands
and how my gaze held you then
in the soft sticky pain of your eyes
while N picked a fight and temper-tantrumed
and in a flash I saw myself at twenty,
my own inability to love
gathered into one foul gesture,
and still I seem to be watching the two of you,
                    my gaze drinking you in,
your eyes almost touching mine,
                    you, my soft undrunk elixir.

Group Portrait, Delft, Late Sixteenth Century.

They opened the dikes five times that year to flood the land.
Cities were torched, the inhabitants bound and gagged,
then forced at lance-point into the frozen canals.
I was executing yet another portrait of the public trustees of an
      orphanage
that their bald correctly-laced presences might shine
in remote museums a thousand years hence.
I enjoy the delicate way their hands rest on the title deeds
for these most Christian places
even as the order "No prisoners" passed along both sides
or another cannonade ripped through the munitions factory
burying in rubble the girls' school for genteel deportment.
Each year the orphanages increased.
The portraits grew heavier and heavier.
The regents must have thought they would lug the weight of them
into the other world.
Nice money if you can get the work
and no one questioned motives:
fidelity to realistic details
right up to the end of the earth.

These stone embankments that look like Venice but they're not Venice,
here where the dark river finds its terminus,
where the ship's prow seeks a tomb among the currents.
Every day, as I paint,
winter water shivers under the footbridge.
The gaunt trees shelter their starved layer of birds:
at each level they define a new habitation.
I once captured the local birds in a biblical triptych:
those rounded brutal mouths shaped by the one cry of begging,

stuffing everything visible into their darkening crevasse.
I wanted to paint as bluntly
as words spoken during an avalanche
yet all's this inevitable smooth,
these muted blues that are the fashion of the age
recording everything precisely as it is:
each official, each battle, the new-born child,
the fruits on the table, the windmill on the hillside to the left
at every change of season –
that's what they wanted and I could do it,
making present to the touch
each thing as it passes into amnesia.

Today at the abandoned Cathedral
the Italian master continues his rehearsals.
No one notices how there's a wobbling at the core of his music
and no matter how high the dancers kick their heels
they will never find solid ground.
The goodly burghers will follow the streamers
and no one thinks twice of the five servant girls
penned in their cages
awaiting the sentence of beheading
for certain lewd practices
as reported by their illustrious employers.
Each day the ocean grows outside the dike.
The wounds in the sky slowly multiply.
Ever more threatening the viking ships come closer.
I continue these stern faces, hands folded in laps,
apocalypse near Delft, the circle sealed.
Long needles knit the great cloaks for our third winter in the
                    trenches.
The troops of the Duke of Alba torch another outlying settlement
while the regents' faces betray no emotion.

They know the civilization I smear on this canvas will last a thousand years.

The Transformation Boat

Just an old plain boat travelling the coastline
and wherever it came to rest its prow against the wharf
from small town to small town
life suddenly would arrive in people's houses.
Dogs and children would stir around midnight
touched by the light that comes from there,
a wavering across all that darkness.
Thin stars would penetrate the hands of businessmen
and make them give away all their belongings
and enter into the fire
or a woman would walk out of a house at dawn
and wake next standing in the souk at Marrakesh,
her midriff spangled in gold, dancing in ecstasy,
her twining arms freed to the sky's rapture.

The boat would glide into the harbour at midnight
and sail off before dawn
and in the plaza of the quiet town
a thin girl would be rolling a hoop at sunset
while other children dart in and out of doorways,
sheltering behind bushes and tall mysterious garbage bins,
playing at gangsters and police,
and all the time
the boat's sails grew steadily like a shadow in their minds.

Someone said Odysseus was on board
and if you stood before the skipper's wheel at full noon
you'd see the crew were Circe's swine rooting their noses in swill.
Another said it was the Flying Dutchman,
another the boat to the Fortunate Isles.

In plain day without leaving anywhere
a girl at the sink draining pasta would kneel to receive the lord.
A small wren would speak from the freezer section of the supermarket
and I would take my fear of breakage and walk forward steadily
the way dreams do.

When the boat left, someone saw water tumbling out of the sky —
a boy recorded how midsummer snow
was falling across the outback.
And all that blocks us from loving would pass away
like mist over glass
and our hands, wiped clean of every line,
could begin at last their journey to the sun.

Turtles

Lost with swollen rats in the grove of banana palms
by the river
older than our solitude

encased in a silence so complete
they forget they carry the bitterness
of earth's memories

in summer as in winter
with such clear eyes
they are swimming towards me.

Paralysis
(1955)

Laid out flat
in the back of the station wagon my father borrowed
I look up:
the leaves are immense,
green and golden with clear summer light
breaking through –
though I turn only my neck
I can see all of them
along this avenue that has no limits.

What does it matter
that I am only eyes
if I am to be carried
so lightly
under the trees of the world?
From beyond the numbness of my strange body
the wealth of the leaves
falls forever
into my small still watching.

Everyday

You go to a restaurant and you eat a meal and you choke and die. It
happens like that. You feel horny and visit a sauna, get careless, catch
aids and die. You open a present while straphanging on a tram, miss
your stop, get off in a hurry, don't notice a truck, get hit and die. Or
you breathe the mould of your own body for a lifetime, day after
silent day, and you turn white and die. Or you open your hand and the
lines suddenly go walking off in different directions over the edges
of the world and this puzzles you and you can't understand it and out
of such perplexity you die. One day the face of the sunflower deity
is splattered on the bedsheets and you grow prickly and are never
visited by the bees that carry sweetness in their thighs and from the
hunger for their soft release you die. You construct a house of stone
underneath a well of pure skywater and there you bring the pillars
of every deity and the offerings for every cult and you crush flowers
and the tiny hands of the newborn dead till reincarnating as gesture
without body you die.

On a Saturday during the football on an airplane over Antarctica in
galoshes in a business suit on the holiday of a lifetime tomorrow and
yesterday after five minutes of thinking and a decade of acceptance
passionlessly as oxygen from a mask in this room which has grown
as small as a child's crib you open your mouth to all that exits and all
that rushes in and wanting so much to speak you start to mime the
opening of a word

and you begin to understand
how the silence that fills you and the passion for words that overflows
is your own private and chaotic death.

Missing Words

I don't know how many things there are in this world that have no name. The soft inner side of the elbow, webbed skin between the fingers, a day that wanders out beyond the tidal limits and no longer knows how to summon the moon it has lost, my firstborn who gazes about himself when the TV dies and there is a strange absence in his world. I was looking for a great encyclopaedia, the secret dictionary of all the missing words. I wanted to consult its index and find out what I could have become. The sound the clock makes when it is disconnected and taken down from the wall but can't lose the habit of trying to jerk itself forward. The look of old socks drying on a rack in the kitchen all through a winter night, hanging starched and sad opposite the wedding photographs. A word for your face when you know you can't love but would almost like to try. The blurred point of merger between fresh storm damage to a house and the deep fissures that have always been there. Walking down the corridor to the front door with inexplicable elation in my chest as if everything was about to start, as if my love had just arrived, escaped from a burning world, and at the same time clenched in my taut wrists, my hands, the thin bones of my arms, the certainty that everything has long been over.

I Want to See the World Beginning
(For Louis, aged four)

In the earthly world the first day is opening.
Turtledoves, tortoises, shy bright-coloured birds,
thin trees that stammer in wind shaking their topmost leaves,
faces half-glimpsed in the passionfruit vine's entrails
and countless other animals still without names:
here on the path that bends
below branches heavy with summer.

Grey-green the lake shines towards us
opening the leaves of each season.
The sun of origins spins in a sky always free of the judgements of men.
Clouds converse among themselves and pay no heed
to the wandering band of their would-be interpreters.
The roundness of day and night, of apples, horizon, homecoming,
is all one circle,
one ever-expanding room
where the walls let our hands glide safely through.

Up ahead
the path leads out beyond forests and paths.
At this point words have made very little headway.
Here no one hoards the grains of the future.
In the heart's pockets a few simple goals:
to be tall the way mountains are,
to leave our fingerprints on the sky.

Where the road curves out of sight
the end of the earth is waiting.
I rush towards it,
my empty arms swinging free.

Japanese Poet on the Train to the Medellín Prison

She enters the train –
enters a green landscape they are tunnelling through,
the silver pebbles of rivers,
sky of the cordilleras.
Her poems are budding slowly
on long streamers of many colours
she thinks she might unleash
in bright air above the prison.
Squid have entered these poems
and the leaves of mulberry trees.
Department stores have entered these poems
and snowfall over Kyoto
and the passionless gaze of boys in pachinko parlours.

Her dress is red and white.
She thinks she could almost be again
a young girl on coming-of-age day –
but today she is travelling
to enter the male prison alone,
to walk down the corridor of tattooed men,
to sit in the wire cage that is open to the sky
and she will let go these wild birds
she has brought with her for the gods of these mountains.

There are things so good the earth takes them:
luminous faces of white and yellow flowers in Spring,
the lips that seek our lips, the mouth that drinks us –
but what do you give the Central Juvenile Detention Centre of Medellín

where the addicts and housebreakers and rapists
and dumb hired killers
who couldn't even get their hits right
are all doing time?
What calligraphy from the mountains of Japan
do you bring for them?
What hidden path is there across the wildest ocean
to connect these lush green valleys of misery
with her secret Temple for lost cats,
her palace of the single perfect kite?
What can her singing
bring to them?
Even in the tropics they are cold at night
but she won't offer them her breasts
to let them shine under the knife blade.
She could imitate the local poets
and simply say "Freedom" over and over.
She could imitate a sisterhood
from the northern land of success
and croon a multitude of cacophonous voices,
a slit throat of broken words.
But today is not like any other day.
Even as she adds fresh symbols to complicate an image
she is conscious her poem is a tree
shedding innumerable leaves.
She is a woman aged fifty-five
shedding her years,
unlearning the grace of a warrior,
giving back the coming-of-age day,
returning the Emperor's scroll.
Writing her poem,
the images no longer fall on the page —
only her wrists move, miming the air.

She doesn't know how she could measure
any poem against the rapist and the murderer
and the crack dealer whose tattooed arms she has seen
over and over in the brief film footage
of the prison she will visit shortly.
She has brought an apple wrapped in a green handkerchief.
She doesn't know what part of the poem it is.
She doesn't know if this is lunch
or seed of her country she has brought to spill among men,
a peace offering to the bewildered
complete otherness
of a young boy wielding an axe against his playmate.

And she has brought sachets of green tea
and paper of five colours for each of the five continents
and with each passing minute of the train trip
her poems have shed another layer.
Her wrists curve as she writes and unwrites
and she thinks of Jeanne Hébuterne, Modigliani's lover,
who threw herself to her death from the fifth-storey window
of the same apartment block she once lived in
and she thinks of wrists as beautiful as hers
threading themselves through glass,
and knows she doesn't have a word to offer anyone

and she will sit – she sees it now – on the bare floor
and unwrap the exquisite parchments she will sing
scarcely glancing at any of them,
and though she imagines herself
releasing them all to the winds,
she will fold them up when it is over
and tie them with cloth
and put them away

and she will sing whatever she can sing
in the darkness of the single cell
obliterated by the light
in all the heat and all the misery and all the evil
that is our earth.

Nine Ways of Writing an American Poem

1.

If you put
                your hand
                                in fire
it hurts.

2.

Knoxville Idaho Nebraska Angel Falls
South Linesville Bridge
and Louisiana
                especially Louisiana

as Pa said on the slow road,
                                "That's it."

or two skunks mating under a chainsaw's shadow
                in Alabama twenty winters ago

by knocking about
                you learn a thing
                                or two.

3.

He put it in me
and he said, Suck
Suck harder

Suck it harder
and he put his fist in my eye
and it hurt.

4.

Writing to Tashkent promptly on odd-numbered days
is a good recipe for peptic ulcers.
All of Cicero's best pupils received straight A's but did they rule empires?
Sometimes an exercise book will open in a sandwich bar in New Brunswick.
By travelling around limestone caves Hieronymus Bosch's cousin
encountered miasmas of snowflake dispensers.
If you are breezy enough we'll all come back without problems
and who can say we don't have the best seats for walking on clouds.
Summer requires that all cats immediately empty their ashtrays and address
their closest human as Frou-frou.
It is essential that adjectives fill spaces as coyotes hunt kinkajous
in the arboreal autumn.
When you open a stone, twilight will bark ferociously on the nearest corner.
Do you know Hausa? Can you spell that in Urdu?
Numbers equate only as optimistically as rocks gather peppermint sticks.
The foot is alien to the subway as the eye is innocent of autopsies.
A full page is better than an empty line.

5.

      Open paratwang

                        of helio-

trope in

        door-

way

              en-

              TRANCE

6.

You take the stick of wood
and slice it carefully
            down the centre
as smooth as you can
then you take each half
and place them
carefully
in one of the two piles.

7.

Fall rises softly in the hamlets of South Dakota.
The prairie dog roils in mid-Catskill umbrage.
I don't know how many roads
have lead me to this house
but it is a house
and it is a road.
I walk on it delicately
with two feet

and it takes me
to a place I have never been
but always dreamed of.

8.

Mallarmé opens his book
and immediately
           as Delacroix once ate oysters in Èze-sur-Loire
I am finding
         CONNECTIONS
Cape Canaveral is Houston is potatoes is pommes frites is
        Oscar Wilde's tombstone lone in the lacework of Père
        Lachaise
under the still spring of the Adirondacks
        Rimbaud on the high road
with the angels dressed in cowboy suits
We were all Zorros twenty haciendas away
skating on that immaculate summer ice of Greenland

At twenty seven
I still wore a tie with a green stripe in the centre
and on "see-saw summer nights"
not far from Wynnesville
where Chagall's violin played in the strawberry dance halls
and all the onion-domed churches of Moscow
kept pealing the first blush of childhood in red satin

mais où sont-les. . .?

Not far from Smithsville
          the road curves to the left

and then curves back to the right.
If you stop there
you will find a gas station
a post office
two banks
three diners
and a building that used to be a department store,
                    then a motel, and is currently up for sale.
When it was a department store we used to buy things there
as did most people.

Hemingway Pound Scott Fitzgerald   my cousin Elie
my best friend in fourth grade, Max
and my dog, Sam
all came this way
or they might have
                    if they had only
                                        stopped.

9.

Here where the angel of unknowing rips from the jawbone's incandescence
calling in the long bonfires
a last first breathless haul away from the space
we all enter in the midstream's cicuitry of fire

as the lone birds carol in unison
this unscrolled catalogue of the bleeding obvious
and the fire almost breaks from the fingertips
in one last desperate lifesurge
and the water almost falls in one miraculous drop from the faucet

If you look closely enough in the dry bonetalk of the hillside
grassblade, rat spoor, pine needle,
the upended radishes of becoming

the mortal wound opens
and the bear goes back to his bearness.

What the Painter Saw in Our Faces (Excerpts)

The painter is shaping what he sees from such a great distance.
The light comes towards him from birth,
from the white operating theatre,
the curtains parted with the outline of dawn across the harbour.
The newborn child, the first-born, is focussing the light.
Other galaxies have bent it
and passed it on.
It carries something stronger
than time or space.
It breaks into the fingers as they uncurl,
into the eyes clear and remote
as they stretch out quite suddenly towards us.

The painter is shaping the light that comes
from the end of our millennium.
In his eyes the patterned floor in a far off kitchen
remakes itself –
like the computer image of a photo
gradually layering itself out
till it is a photo,
an image of something contemporaneous but delayed.
So the hollow cheek of the woman
whose world is burning
glances up into the camera.
All the valley behind her is defecated with loss –
tents shredded by wind,
people snatched away in the night,
a pram left behind on the slope that is smouldering.
She is crying.
No one has bothered to translate her words.

The camera has moved somewhere else.
Yet from so far off
the painter knows how the light is shaped by her.

There is a light even stronger
that comes from the place further off
where quiet has descended on the winter valleys
and smoke rises, twisting and curling,
from the villages beyond the river
and already the man with the lyre has gone,
the girl fishing has gone,
the silver trays of food prepared for the marriage feast
all gone.
An immense silence rises from the laneways and villages.
The same green and white signs hang from awnings
over the freeways.
The signs shadow us into villages and cities
that no longer exist.
Whatever comes from there has suffered
an extraordinary bending.
It carries the silence
of trees without birds,
apartment blocks detonated and smouldering,
the hillside where five hundred men stand
waiting to be shot one by one.

What kind of animal are we?
The animal that wounds its own kind.
The animal that only loves through wounding.

In the landscape claimed by the people of the wolf
frescoes of half a dozen churches
scattered across several valleys

sold to the young men in the cafes
bought in one breath
by the young men laughing and smoking and drinking
shots of rum to chase down the beer
and the girlfriend nodding her head to the rock music
smiles into the camera:
"Yes, we'd die for that."
Their leather jackets, their mobile phones
hum quietly in the evening air,
reckless, defiant,
waiting for the first bombs of that night.
So we trade our life for a falsehood –
so we line up people against a wall in the name of dead stone,
so we excise a lover
suddenly after breakfast because that's what you do.

And those in the small hamlets
who didn't know if there was a next village
or if the sun knew any fields beyond their valley
or if water only bloomed for them –
the pitchforks at their throats, the jeepload of drunken militia,
the spray of machine guns in the stalls
where the roosters lay bloody and scattered,
leaving only in their clothes, no food, no water,
told – *There, look, it's that way,*
get walking –
and they didn't think to ask what *it* was called,
there where they had to walk,
night's drizzle already coming down
and the cold dark of the mountains where wolves lived
and the bombs under the earth that took half the children
and the fear of whatever groups they would meet
there where no laws exist, no customs, no known parameters –

their only clue that they must always be heading up,
the dawn sun at their backs, the setting sun in their eyes
and scooping the water from drains
and the sores from the wet wrappings on their legs exploding
and the dead, white-haired and tender,
gracing the loneliness of earth in the fields where they laid them.

And the masters of the world have nothing to offer death
but death,
lightly letting it slip from their hands,
wounding become mechanical gesture
as if you could hurt the world into compliance.

*　　*　　*

Is this a portrait of marriage?
The bridegroom's face totally rapt, his eyes almost crying
yet his gaze fixed not on the bride, not even the other women,
but in the sky above.
As if intense love is always a looking up.
Both hands pluck the harp his eyes have forgotten.
And on the hill behind him
the twined garlands of marriage,
two sheets laid out, crumpled by future lovemaking,
two large womb-shaped bowls ripe and full.
Red drapery hangs from the tree
that they might enter into love clothed only in flame –
that their marriage be green of the earth,
red of passion, gold of divine silence.
And the two girls, bridesmaids perhaps, gaze attentively at him.
The snake is almost invisible. It curves in the grass.
The woman who has seen it stands transfixed –
as if, though some distance from it still,

she already surrenders to its bite
and welcomes it as singly as the husband
welcomes heaven in his gaze.
So that each tumbles into some chasm of the self,
precisely there
where all the symbols are of giving.

Did the painter mean this for me?
Where my sleep is one continuous dipping and floating
gasping for the breath of you.

Who are we? Where are we going?

That night you sat crying in the restaurant,
Help me, help me, you said,
and I didn't know what to say or do,
my kisses useless, our hands unable to save each other,
the rain outside falling enormous, constant.
What you held in your eyes, under your skin
was your death,
small and clear and unarguable.
I couldn't lift it from you
and as I listened and watched
and again and again
brushed your face with my lips,
your phone kept ringing
connecting you to a drowned continent
that you kept trying to hold
only each call died away from you
and, when each voice stopped, the pain throbbed more than ever.
You had wounded yourself again that afternoon
burning the soft skin between your elbow and wrist
and you blew a child's tear-moistened breaths across it

while you talked to me and the invisible others
in a vast abandonment I couldn't reach.
I took you to bed but that didn't help.
I would walk with you across the sky but that didn't help.
Beloved in your distant land,
your land of exile and of loss,
the drums of your Africa you played once
are stilled now
and all the slave memories your wounded body carries
and the chorus of birds you laid across bright tiles
are shattered in the dust-clouds of this war
you re-enact upon your body
and that no one knows how to stop.

In the train carriage a man is writing a letter in Arabic:
that script you loved so much:
his hand curving an infinite line on the void.
My lover with green eyes,
my lover with hair white as the sands of the beaches that ring your
        island,
your words curve out against the void.
Ignoring the horizon's red-grey tinge
later we'll skip through the rain
and your fingers will find their way again under my clothes
as I kiss you,
our time running out by the second.

*   *   *

The light from the doorway is presence.
It floods towards us.
Suddenly it has the gold-rimmed form
of a kindly, slightly crotchety man,

an artist, Vermeer perhaps
or Velazquez or Nicolas Poussin,
as he might have been remade by chance
through the random jumbling of all atoms
in an alternate world governed by other models of time.
And as the door behind him stays open
we see his face tilt towards us,
his brush silently
mixing the hues our earth has yet to discover.

Why do you want to paint us?
We are going down into darkness.
What draws you to our shapes?

With the road lost again where the buildings loom,
if not a painter from another galaxy
who could be saving us?
Beyond the coastlines
out there in the oceans that separate us
there plunges and spurts among icy waters
some creature so large we could be its dreams,
our puny viciousness
some inflammation of its skin that will subside quite easily
when the delicate skein of another million years
lies tangled among swaying algae
and the tall spikes of budding corals.

Since we will be no more
what does it matter?
You asked me that night, "Why must I die?"
Over and over it was your question.
It caught somewhere between our tongues as we kissed.
It writhed like a third partner

slithering between our arms,
stinging us back from the edges of pleasure.
"I have done nothing wrong, why must I die?"
The death imprinted deep inside your body
was growing every minute like a child
whose voice kept breaking from your lips
in the same bewildered words.
And there was no answer I could make –
nothing that could help,
not conversation not kisses not lovemaking,
and yet you gave me that night
all of the earth in your hands.

"I don't want to be famous after I die", you said,
interrupting whatever I might have been thinking,
breathing the deep honey of your body.
"I just want to live."
And you turn your face from the painter's eye
as from the cruelty of the lens.
Yet the painter understands your reluctance.
He erases the biographies.
The painter has lost all our names:
he is more interested in that moment
when a man stoops to tie his shoelaces, there at the street-corner,
or in the vein-darkened hand of the woman, in the savagery of her
            wrist
fighting back the tangles of her hair.
He is simply praying,
Let this paint be the kiss no earthly lover
knows how to give,
Let the colour in this green of your upward glancing,
almost trusting eyes
brim with all the tenderness life never gave you.

And the shore has so many souls,
all rightfully timid of the water
and their strangely shy nudity under the single
                              tied sheet that covers them
and the conch shell in the hands of Orpheus,
who has abandoned his lyre forever
as he sanctifies the waters,
sounds as a new language,
fresh and growing in their ear.

                    *   *   *

Just sleep, my love. The river has surrounded us.
The severed hands have floated out to sea.
On the high chalk banks
the children stand laughing and shy
leaping and nudging each other
to watch the gods drift by
as they leave the earth for ever, floating past
across the whirlpools and eddies
of another age gone by.
The river rising will lap against your hair, your face.
I am bone fingers.
I am the brittleness of all that breaks.

At the frontier
on the bald hillside
the gates, silent now, are wedged together
with chains and blocks of wood.
The empty rooms are multiplying.
Inside the empty barracks and frontier posts
the cracked ice weeps softly under the doors,
tears itself away from all it has known

and joins the river which flows down from the mountain.
The secret valley, promised, denied,
slept in after all
for one night and always
is there in the cupped creases
of your hand
fallen open in sleep.
I do not know your name –
how can I say it?

They have come with a scanner to issue people names
and with plastic cards to give people back their identity
or let them choose one
or invent one
now the world has gone away from them.
They are building a metro station
there at the frontier camp,
there at the highest point of the mountain ridge
where all the rivers of the earth have their origin.
A⭙IRO⭙ ⭙EN⭙D⭙C⭙IO
Unlimited Hotel/Enormous Refuge for Strangers
they have called it,
that the language of Orpheus
may take this pain and transform it.

Not so easy our lives.
Wind scours the empty rooms,
the tables, the chairs, the camp beds,
all the refuse let fall behind the buildings.
A cup of coffee was burning on the table
where it had stayed on alone –
the afternoon gathering the uncertain
insignia of rainclouds,

behind me the city you had walked through so many times
that I would soon leave forever
and, lightly brushing your eyes,
a burnt text of sadness almost,
the Arabic newspaper left abandoned on the table opposite.

A kiss – a world destroyed – all taken back.

On the chalk banks
where the snake of the river slithers rapidly towards the sea
the children release their kites
fluttering and rising over everything.
A single line stood on the ancient wall,
its curved script dotted with interrogation.
You could read nothing
yet you felt its presence.
The house that had fallen once
would fall again.
This graceful line travelling
from right to left across the void,
moving crabwise backwards to its source,
all its flourished refinement now only
a hand marking the death tally.

Beyond the snowline
stakes mark out an ancient vineyard reclaimed by crows.
Maybe you walk there now among the crows
on the high edges where rivers begin –
maybe it's the same river the artist was painting
with the world in flames on the other bank, some tributary
that later will carry old ramparts and smoking villages
in its depths,
resting silent a moment here

where your hermitage is hidden.
Your motor stopped,
you step among rocks by the roadside,
your jacket hunched around you in the cold,
breathing a cigarette as your eyes frame the scene
in one last photo.

That night at a table across from us,
fresh from his wheeling and dealing,
the businessman carousing two women
glares mockingly across at us,
the two of us thin and haggard as junkies,
shaking and weeping the cold
of our last night together on this earth,
and the women beside him half embarrassed half fascinated
by the sly outrageous crassness of his taunts
and none of them knowing, as they nursed
the long green twilight of their swirling drinks,
that the glass had already shattered,
its thousand fragments flung wide
some of them lodging deep inside us,
your face already come open like a flower,
your hands opening into my hands,
slivers of the mirror of this world
scarred into our throats,
nicking traces of remote stars
at the turning of the elbow,
caressing a red line halfway up your thigh
where my lips would brush against it and weep

and as we walked out of the restaurant into night
leaning our woundedness against each other
rain was falling with its debris of other lives.

The war seemed quiet that night —
only its banners dismantled by the wind
shredded themselves around the spikes
of desecrated flagpoles.
In a shopfront window a lone TV talking to itself
showed other villages torched and burning
there beyond the river.
A tiny cockroach
almost not quite born
mechanically stuttered its first shiverings of antennae
along the rim of a drain.
That night — every night those months.

Everything indicated that the end had come.
The river had packed and freighted
its cargo of survival.
Water, once spoken to,
no longer boiled.
The women had moved their tents beyond the snowline.
The crows assembling pecked at broken glass.
Fragments of death like stone
lay in the water.
The sky, cradled its whole life
by the twin arms of river and ocean,
shivered at the caress of stone and glass.
I watch you leave forever from your other world
only a little less distant than the moon,
the last time of closing a suitcase,
the last time of your hand in its mechanical tiredness
grasping soap,
the last time for the pressure of light from the open hotel window,
its shutters drawn back against grey morning,
light that is flooding you for the last time,

holding your face with all its pain
for the last time
yourself not knowing as you fold the clothes
as the time in your travelling clock runs out
as the room leaves you
yourself hesitant, confused and tender
in all the light that sheathes your body
fragrant with the lovemaking of all your life
as you go to the window and the day explodes
shattering you, shattering its fragments
into you
and the world ends.

Parable of the Two Boxes

In the small box what do you hold?
Self-righteous evil

In the large box what do you hold?
A great emptiness

With what do they make the small box?
Out of lives out of breath out of living

With what do they make the large box?
Out of what is left over from the small box
Out of what was too invisible to be made into the small box

Can you describe what you see when you open the small box?
Two heads with one face
A normal whispering of words
Perhaps the small clink of power

Do you see that or hear that?
Seeing is hearing when things are small enough.

And the large box — what do you see inside that?
Earth, lots of earth, I run my hands through it, it is warm in places
like ashes have been ploughed into earth, like cities have bled into it,
and glass and bones have dissolved there

Could you give a word for the large box?
It is what is done to us

Is there a word for the small box?

No – yes, it is what happens. Perhaps it is what a large number of emptinesses do to save themselves when they are still at the point of wanting to save themselves

What temperature is the large box?
Cold, very cold

What temperature is the small box?
Also cold, but there are small glints of burning as well

What else is in the room?
Nothing

If you mixed the boxes what would happen?
They would go back to being themselves – it is their nature

What can you do then?
Yes, what can you do?

Scavenger

Working down the river and the sunlight
he gathers plastic bags
he gathers old drink bottles
the tops of beer cans
old sticks the wind leaves
from the trees he gathers cobs of spring
the pine cones
and the river's muddy presence
is the sacred place of scavenging

he is perhaps a bird lost on land
his eyes sharp as a bird's
thin and eloquent in bones
tall and straight as a stork moving
through mangroves or the dark dredge of grey-green leaves
for the bower he doesn't build
for the little ones not there to feed
in spaces of shelter under winter's sky
as the tall trees lean into his face
his simplicity is angular
he goes before us
he shares our fate
but with an angry jerkiness
naming my face among his enemies
like an eagle with a twisted leg
in his wild stare the human tribe knows itself
as only ever conditionally at peace

brother I can't approach
in this sunlight that blesses and absolves
while the river's scarred bending
tilts him further and further
beyond the thin blurred line of unreachableness
all the wind brings
torn kite-strings the cloudscape of the hills
promises of early spring
the river turning brown under the trees
that a moment before looked almost blue with summer
the code of lost and misdirected letters
the ego's madness
and in his bag is what is left from our lives.

Why the Minotaur is Always Sad

So many years underground,
his head dizzy from bumping all those memory-clouds.
Always to be the centrepiece
of someone else's puzzle.
His endless consumption of women
didn't help much.
And so this morning he has arrived in his kingdom:
a wise gathering of rocks,
a little girl trying to paint flowers on the pebbles
but the waves keep washing them clean,
his chair opposite the ocean,
the tree with its gaze that says
    "I too have lived elsewhere."

Apologia Pro Vita Sua

One night in Paris I saw glowing in a small shopwindow a page of René Char's handwriting: *Recours au ruisseau*. The delicate ink of finality. At the foot of the poem I saw where Char had dated it – three years and two days before my birth. At that hour the backstreet, somewhere between the Musée d'Orsay and Opéra, was completely deserted. Lit by a single light-bulb, the window seemed to have waited over half a century to find me.

Last night I dreamt again of my own death. Guided by the head priest of some strange church I was ascending the inner staircase of an immense tower, just ahead of me my family and the serene and tender face of the Buddhist poet, my friend Judy. We marvelled at the wall we were climbing against – a magnificent rust-red patterned in waterpipes, putti and other embellishments of the underworld. With my crippled leg and damaged body I had fallen behind the others when a stair broke, the cracked stone slab crashing into the darkness below. I woke on a stretcher inside the church. The priest had bandaged me and removed my calliper and I lay there praying that I would stand and walk again. In the poem Char promises that he will "begin again higher up", that when all is destroyed the river will speak. The priest's voice flowed on, a darkened stream in which I could recognise no reflection but which held, I sensed this strongly, no malevolence. Weighed down by his robes of office he was simply doing what he could, human and divine, to summon a miracle. Impatient to rejoin my family I tried to put the calliper back on but my fingers no longer knew how to grasp laces or buckle straps.

I rested at the top of a low hill where the dry yellow grass folded around me. In the distance, unreachable now, was a small stream that divided me from the others. The magic rites of the church were beginning to take effect as I woke again in the air a little way above myself. The panic of not being there for my children came and went in waves like a long cargo ship buried in the shadow of bridges, like everything else abandoned to its own fate.

I remembered the flooded world of Char's landscapes, barges gliding through villages and under fortified walls, and that beautiful word *l'amont*, "upstream". I remembered the confident builder he was, defiant of all downfalls. I was already dead and I was still only just underway.

Some Mountains

The mountain beyond that pass has no name. It is too old for us to name it. The sea has the same colour as the sky but the mountain has the same colour as sand. Sand is not earth but a fluid shoreline that leads to the great cities. When we are tired we buy up land on the edges of the great cities so we can sit and watch the insomniac journey of sand. Its slow exodus across the horizon teaches us how to prepare for sleep. When flowers open on a day filled with sand all the water in the world will not quench their thirst.

I send words to you from so far off aiming to shape you towards the exquisite openness of love, but over and over I collapse in the effort to invent a life. Walking on sand has taught me I can no longer count on making it to any shore. Your eyes as I imagine them I will go on kissing gently and sheltering beneath. It may be that simply wishing you such tenderness will help you wake one day calmer, more deeply held by the world's alignment, ready to find another and love. We cannot name sandgrains or some mountains but perhaps they can name us.

Where the Roads Go After Nightfall

Sometimes a road bends in darkness,
bends from the sheer weight of travelling
across the line into night.
The river hurled under you,
like a great doubt below bridges,
may be there or not.
The stars curve away
and all that life meant –
the naked sweetness of the sky –
disappears with the vanished signposts.
So still, the most distant hills
and the earth just in front of you are one.
You stand on a different path then
getting used to the empty sky
as it wraps itself about you,
getting used to the worm food,
to the blindness of walking without eyes.
The rush the dead must feel
bleeds suddenly into you
and the unimaginable grows inside you
as a fire can burn for years inside itself
giving out only darkness.

Lonelier worlds stretch endlessly out there:
your feet have taken their first step
into that space:
where the roads go after nightfall.

Apologising to Unicorns

Apologising to unicorns is problematic. They rarely understand our purposes. Tenderness will often be seen as the manipulative gestures of a fear that seeks death – for itself and others. Unicorns sleep most comfortably in heavy traffic where the hum of self-absorbed commuters leaves them invisible. To find a unicorn in a forest is like falling asleep in English and waking up fluent in Pashtun. Someone may well have done it. Unicorns sense above all our uncertainty of ourselves, our not belonging, our poor talent for letting the miraculous be. Stripped back to primal desecration, our hearts still yearn for unicorns. We trail our clouded mirrors in the waters of sky-stretched ponds. Although they will never look to us for food or shelter unicorns are reluctant to abandon their legend of our existence. Our one virginity is that we are not yet born.

Of Poetry

Great poems are often extraordinarily simple.
They carry their openness
with both hands.
If there is a metaphor lounging in a doorway
they step briskly past.
The boom of generals
and presidents with their rhetoric manuals
will go on sowing the wind.

The great poems are distrustful of speech.
Quietly,
like someone very old
who has only a few hours left of human time,
they gaze into the faces around them –
one by one
they kiss love into our mouths.

Reading Borges, Late at Night and Imagining Buenos Aires

1.

No one dreams the river as it is.
If I transpose sides
and make new islands,
if I annex one shore
and tie it to another continent,
it is only to remind myself that here is all places.

Nightfall, the concrete slit where snow-melt
and drains from dull backyards
all merge as mud,
the blue lines of maps
like the sky was sketching its own arteries.
No one dreams the river as it is.

2.

I never left the airport.
All I could see
were the lines of light marking the edges
of the harbour.
The metal detectors
went wild as I passed through and two soldiers
trained their machine guns at me
as my arms shot up
in gesture of surrender.
Imagining Buenos Aires from the air.

Lines of light at 2 am
giving the vague curve of river and bay.
I spent hours trying to find change
small enough for the drink machine.
City of Borges and of tangos,
of Palermo, the Recoleta
and the Plaza de Mayo.

Imagining Buenos Aires from the airport lounge:
its décor of posters
(more snowfields of the Andes, more seals),
the internationally flavoured
minidrinks of its bar.
Imagining Buenos Aires from a book of poems
written from the unimaginable year of my father's birth
to the time I turned sixteen –
City of Borges and of tangos,
of Palermo, the Recoleta and the Southside,
of Serrano and the Plaza de Mayo.
Paris of the South,
where are you?

Almost not a sound in all that space.
Cold after the tropics. I imagine a plain of darkness
stretching endlessly beyond the terminal's walls.

City that will never quite make dawn,
I image you as night
and night you stay.

3.

There are days when watches stop,
years when time runs backwards.
My son's voice, my daughter's voice
reach me,
a faint whispering sliding across
the thousand thousand miles of ocean.

I wake and sleep
entrusting all my body
to a room whose name
is Departure.

4.

What was beauty, what was pride
lost in our multiple hands.

In the grainy substance of the documentary
a shadow walks beside Maria Kodama
stroked by the city's tremulous sun
or a voice intones «*Sólo del otro lado del ocaso*"
on the faded tape playing in a car radio
as my son zigzags his way across a soccer field,
the rain sluicing down.

My ancestors roamed the world
leaving Ireland for California, for Dunedin, Melbourne,
the always elsewhere gold
that became treachery and war,
names that echo like Junín or Anzac Cove,

so many young men's bodies
under a limpid sky.

5.

To spin
like the globe gone wild.
To drift across continents
like reluctant rainclouds.
To arrive
a voice pale as last year's ashes.

To claim membership
in the illustrious confraternity of ghosts.
To cross in a loop
the Southern Pole.
To dream our lives have passed
in an endless prolongation of night.

6.

A maid's hands
straighten the blinds in a hotel room
I never stayed in.
Taxi doors open and close
on a trip I never took.
Imagining Borges imagining Buenos Aires –
the labyrinth of streets and names,
the infinite library of first moments.
Shuffling days out of an itinerary
and waking late one afternoon

on a city's outskirts –
the cantinas, the dirt, the sky –

to stumble
face-forward
into a heart attack or a stranger's knife

to claim this destiny
where all depends on never
stepping through a doorway.

7.

Night comes
and poets will climb out of their coffins
and the music will flow:
John Forbes Nazim Hikmet Federico García Lorca
César Vallejo and Yeats and Supervielle
and Wallace Stevens a little aloof
and Whitman at the centre of numerous groups, and Rilke
fuming with the bluster of cigarettes and the silent vibration of angels

and the blind will wonder what skin they are in
and the tormented will find a great quiet
(gently picking the unravelling stitches,
bone that speaks, the pure sun
brought back from its dream of ice:
Elizabeth Bishop, Sylvia Plath and Alejandra Pizarnik;
Señor Borges rolling the patience of syllables
between an absent finger, an absent thumb)

and many will sit quite still
knowing the sea has moved endlessly through them
and a few will turn over stones
that break up into words in their hands.

It will go on
the way it would if there were no walls
as if this life was made
from only our breath.

8.

love and the rain that falls in an unspoken miracle

windows opening on a harbour where the lights continue burning long
    after dawn

the last day in a city you will never return to, saying goodbye to its
    trees, how the drink in a bar goes on trembling lonely in its glass

midday in the drowned city, the facades of buildings scooped up in a
    handful of water

a painting in which everything has been included: a painting from
    which everything has been left out: the same painting

9.

When a breeze comes
and a spider travels upside down
across the ending of the hottest day in Autumn,

I drop into a cool quiet zone
which is the possibility of writing.
East of here
all of South America is making breakfast –
measuring bottled water for the coffee
that will be yesterday.
Shadows of ancestors, possibilities of being
move round me as I write,
cut off by the universal script of night.

10.

So many years adding on,
marking the slow
encroachment of perfection
but living would be beautiful
drinking the still-standing water
in the tall glass
that mirrors the world.

From Apocrypha Book I

XVII

Anaximenes was the first to calculate accurately the size of the universe. Whereas Nepenthe, daughter of the mathematician Ptarchus, devised the constant for the weight of the sky. Her cousin Mystra proved the different weight of varying dreams. Mystra was the first to show conclusively that dreams of water are far heavier than dreams of fire. When all these great and learned calculations were presented to Sarsus the third, King of Kings and ruler of all Parthia, he remained unimpressed. After all he was a man who for the first twenty-five years of his life had lived in total seclusion, speaking only the language of spells and unaware that any other languages existed. To utter a word, for him, was to make that thing happen. He had difficulty understanding the idea of a language that merely reported what was – for him all words were there to bring things into being.

(Zenobia, *The Chronicles of Parthia and Palmyra*)

Know then of the three great languages. Beyond the Indus developed the language uniquely capable of expressing philosophical speculation and matched to the knotted and intricately curved play of reality. In Greece the true language of poetry arose with its fusion of beauty, power and the precise contours of human endurance. And in the lands of upper Egypt and greater Parthia was born the delicate and terrifying language of magic, the language that brings about whatever is desired to happen. Whilst the languages of Greece and India remain among us and have been well recorded, the language of the Magi and the Invisible Ones never travelled across borders. It was a speech that did not survive because it did not want to survive. Yet numerous are its fragments. It speaks itself in dreams and in water. It translates stars and rivers into birdsong. Once its spells raised cities, united lovers and gave youth back to the dying. But it became a confusion on the road of warriors. It feared the powerful and warlike – so it left earth.

(Macrobius, *Of the Eastern Kingdoms*)

From Apocrypha Book II

V

While travelling with his parents from Alexandria to Ephesus, the young Nicanor experienced something that would change his life. The boat which had been stumbling across the incertitude of ocean put in at an island that had appeared miraculously in previously uninhabited sea. After several days of crowded ship-board existence, rocking monotonously on deck in choppy seas and feeling the harsh poverty of the food, the three of them – Nicanor and his parents – set off to find oranges, for the island was said to have an immense supply of an exquisite blend of this fruit according to the Captain who had abandoned his boat in the port to go off in search of them.

After winding their way uphill for some half-hour, having lost sight of the dock, they realised that the island spoke to them. His parents registered this in the yellowish tinge that entered their eyes though they could not make out the words. Only Nicanor could hear the sounds of the island and follow the intricate delicacy of its speech.

Reaching the top of the hill where it seemed the best oranges were, they turned back to gaze at the sea below only to find their boat was no longer in the harbour. A long jagged wall extended across the island and had been circling them steadily as they walked. From time to time they caught sight of the people who lived on the other side of this wall, and from their stricken appearance it was soon obvious that the island was a giant floating leprosarium. Either from shock or the thirst inspired by their closeness to the oranges, Nicanor entered the deep sleep that protected him. In this sleep he spoke constantly with the island.

Later, when the time was right, he made himself into a statue so he could be taken off the island and finally brought to Ephesus. Of his parents, or the boat, or the other passengers, no record is kept.

(Evander of Kos, *The Pre-History of Nicanor, prophet of the darkness in Ephesus*, Year 12 of the Fourth Eusebian Era)

The wondrous deeds and teachings of Nicanor gave rise to perhaps the most influential of all religions. Two rival versions of his life were recorded – one by the physician Adeodatus and one by his supposed cousin, the High Priestess Ademeter. Nicanor's teachings were particularly taken up on Atlantis during the fourth manifestation of Eusebius. His sermon on the righteousness of wealth found a special resonance with them, given their addiction to property of all kind and their cult of war. The saying "Death to the poor", ascribed to Nicanor in Adeodatus' Life, is translated differently in Ademeter's version as "Let the poor enjoy the depth of their sleep". The paradoxical nature of Eusebius owes much to this religion. How other than by consulting religion can one explain the peculiar ferocity of their addiction to ownership and the elimination of others? On Eusebius they shrunk language so steadily that in the end no one could speak his own name for fear it was the property of another who had perhaps sold it elsewhere to invest in the future of sunrise. But did Eusebius become so warlike and self-destructive because of, or in spite of, the Nicanorean Ethics and the Creed of the Revived Statues of Ephesus? Scholars point out that similar practices arose during the third manifestation of Eusebius among the outer Dacians though not on the same scale, given the underdeveloped nature of the Dacian court system. Possibly, as hostile critics of the Nicanoreans assert, Nicanor's long time in deep sleep and his subsequent life as a statue blinded him to the value of such emotions as love, selfless generosity or artistic pursuits. Possibly the Eusebioli rewrote all the texts. Some suggest that his entire existence was a case of mistranslation.

(Lucian of Gades, *A brief history of the rise of the Nicanoreans*, 858 the alternative calendar)

Fifty years after its first manifestation on the westernmost island of Atlantis, the Kingdom of Eusebius held a secret council to decide whether it should declare itself the World Government. The renowned archons Aegisthus and Menandros spoke in favour of the efficiencies to be gained should direct control be extended where the might of the Eusebian court and the Eusebian compulsory exchange committee already regulated all aspects of life. In this way, they argued, everyone could be more efficiently taxed to fund their own repression. Yet the majority, led on by the religious zeal of a certain Monochrastes, rejected the proposal, claiming such an act would undermine the purity of the Nicanorean faith. How could the principle of non-reciprocity be respected if all people became Eusebioli? Otherness must be maintained, Monochrastes urged, if the sacred duty of exploitation was to be extended to all corners of the galaxies. Likewise it was feared such a gesture might damage morale in the military – troops might be less enthusiastic about exterminating peripherals and non-successful-entities if they too could be called Eusebioli.

(Macronius of Illyria, *The Chronicle of a Sad Kingdom*)

VII

Among the Cimmerians there is a small island, most commonly referred to as Hyperborean Amorgos. The island is riddled with holes, treacherous precipices and caves. Sometimes a lake or river is found underneath, but mostly there is only silence and darkness. The people who live here likewise bear gashes and holes all over their bodies. Often the centre of the hand is missing or it may be possible to look through another's cheek and see the sky. Mostly death awaits these people as it awaits everyone only earlier and more painfully. Yet immortals also live on this island who have learned from the holes in their being to patch together a music that will save them. It is rumoured that the Sirens were women of Hyperborean Amorgos who had been stolen by sailors and left on the Wandering Islands.

The speech of those who dwell on Hyperborean Amorgos is curious. These people speak not one but two languages. In the first every word is built outwards from the simplest stems: earth [uk], air [aauuu], fire [hith], water [gliss]: along with twelve tones that register shifts in one's state of calm or anxiety. This speech they call "building speech" for in it they attempt to cement their longing to endure. The second speech called "hathor" is an alarming discontinuity of grief and rapture. Sometimes they call this "soaring speech". It is possible to explain everything at very rapid speed in this language but it is not a good language to use for cooking soup or preparing fish. Those who are in tune with each other naturally adjust their languages quite easily to achieve harmony while those who clash address each other inappropriately.

The subtle spontaneous modulations of these languages and their penetrating yet eternally flawed mirroring of existence are probably the chief explanation of the Sirens' song – that or the homesickness of women who, never abandoning the chasm through the centre of the chest called love, have gazed beyond death.

(from Dio Cassius, *A true account of the circumnavigation of Europe from Lusitanian Gades to the Chersonese Bosphorus*)

XVIII

The Floriendi are very skilled at visualising and holding onto
    the inward maps for things.
By night they climb down enormous ladders into the space of their
    dreams.
What life intends for them next
is always in the third room on the left.
What they most long for

is in the first room on the right.

When it rains in their land, they float above the downpours
to map the concourse of the rivers.
Like the fingers weary gamblers stretch across a table late at night,
the bones of the rivers of the world cannot see how they all connect.

When the dry season comes the Floriendi unroll their maps.
To a clicked litany of dry grass,
they finger the waterholes.

Beauty and coolness break in the mouths of their dreams.

(from *The Black Book of Ebtesum*)

XX

At the front of our house is dawn
and the mist of the sea that enters our valley.

On tree-branches
the cold dawn-smoke rests:

notes from invisible birds
give the dead back their sleep.

~o~

Stumbling out to watch the dawn
I forget I am lonely.
Two million suns
have still
left room for me.

204

~o~

The most remote land
is present on my balcony
at dawn.

(from *The Green Book of Ebtesum*)

XXVII

To the north
bow low
scatter the beads of water
gently scoop tufts of wheat
let the wind trickle
through emptiness

To the east
bow low
scatter the grains of dawn
may your hands be open
kneel
let where the sun is
know you
Speak
"Shame on my head
on my eyes
Shame on my lips and tongue
Shame on my hands
on my walking
Shame of the seed

and of destiny."
Again dip slowly your hand
into the grain sack
scatter grain
scatter what lives
what will live
Speak
"Grain of grains
dew of sea
fire that rises from mist
accept our shame"
bow again
lightly sprinkle the water

To the south
stand firm that the realms
of Four Heavens
may see you
bow low
scatter the grains
let the ghosts
know of your presence
scatter the dew of water
let the beads of water
rest on the lips of all people
let the thirst of the living
and the thirst of the dead
be calmed
bow again
wait for the silence
to give you permission
to stand

To the west
eyeing the west as an equal
eyeing the west as a mother
eyeing the west as your child
scatter the grain
scatter the bright joy of water
kneel
kneel do not speak
wait for the light that rises and sets
to touch you
wait for the winds that come
from the lands of all the dead
to filter around your ears
wait for their voices to enter you
wait till their voices speak
wait till the words
are fierce and tender
wait till the words
tear at the sinews of pain
till the words slice
through forehead and skull
till the heart is open to all words
the earth is struggling to say

Kneel longer
wait till their voices
cease
wait till the silence steadies you
speak
"Brothers"
speak
"Sisters"
speak

"I give back
I give back
I give back"

(*Dawn Ritual of Purification* for families and descendants of those who participate in slaughter, to be used by all visitors who enter the Holy City of Kitezh)

From Apocrypha Book III

VII

Half an arm's length above me
mosquitoes tracing a zigzag pattern,
unpredictable, elaborate,
more beautiful than stars.

Completely still
I watch the grey swarm's
inexplicable drawing –
tiny masters of life and death,
greetings!

(Erycthemios, *Knowings*, Book IV)

XI

"The blue snail"

It does not offer
an answer
to autumn.

There
where it has dragged
its own sky

everything it touches
shines
with belonging.

~o~

Over a stone bridge
all feet leave their own
residue of mud.

~o~

The vendors of bread and sweet pastries
stalls laden with beads and perfumes
mansions of the rich
sinking yearly deeper into the city's
obliterating mud

And before me
the white butterfly confused by the wind's messages
the plum tree opening its fragrance of coolness.

(*The Green Book of Ebtesum*)

XV

Outside they were burning the blue-veined leaves of the balikbo plant whose smoke clears the air of mosquitoes and the earth of fire-ants but, if once inhaled, its breath fills a man with loneliness, a subtle but disorienting loneliness for which there is no cure. Whoever has tasted deeply of the balikbo plant wanders far from all family. The ants disown him, the mosquitoes shun his presence. As the balkibo's blue-veined breath uncurls within him, he feels the universe take a small but infinite step away from him. He sees his apartness as incurable, his irrelevance to the flow of the world as absolute. Offerings made for him at the temple

consume the fire that is lit for them. His name erases itself from all
language. Truly the world forgets him.

(Sallust, *On African curses*)

XVI

In Kitezh and the kingdoms nearby, though they know of stone and
timber and partly use them as conditions require, they prefer to build
with water. The most prized houses employ three or more interwoven
waterfalls for their walls and the roof is generally left open to the
night sky. In inclement weather sheets of a certain plant painted with
invisibility are used. Sleep, they say, is always deepest when surrounded
by flowing water and the stars glitter with most tenderness when seen
across a ceiling of shifting water. When a couple seek privacy they divert
a waterfall around themselves – "to draw the curtain of the waterfall"
is the common expression in their language to refer to lovemaking.

(Macrobius, *A journey through Ebtesum, Kitezh and central Africa*)

In periods of history when Eusebius has been on the wane or recently
disappeared, following the cyclic collapse of its manifestations, alternate
forms of wealth developed. For too long historians have neglected the
lively trade in water and advanced water technologies that flourished
in Africa. The export of such knowledge from Africa to regions of
Europe, Arabia, and Southern India was crucial to the flourishing of
the twin kingdoms of Kitezh and Ebtesum. Also worthy of further
analysis is the fact that, when Eusebius triumphs, those parts of the
world richest in water become the poorest – a direct punishment, many
hold, for those eras when water regulated the affairs of men. Vast water
distribution highways, of which the aqueducts of the Romans are but
faint memories, linked many lands that the blessings of the fruitful

clouds might be known to all. Likewise the craftsmen of Kitezh and central Africa knew how to use the power of water to run all manner of machines, to transport goods, to lift heavy weights. Many have written of the music created by special water machines, the criss-crossing melodies of water especially prized in Kitezh.

(Diogenes Laertes, *Commentary on Received Knowledge*)

XVII

He is coming,
the great poet of African silences.
Water is in his steps,
the great torrent
of water crashing though rocks,
water that slips and glides
through the locked fingers of children
dreaming of sunlight.
He speaks the soft rain of all seasons,
he speaks the fragrance of fruit,
the drawers and porters of water,
the skilled craftsmen
who shape and guide water
to accomplish all the longings of men.
He speaks the unspoken abundance,
the full granary's ease, the floor laid out
for the ritual greeting,
In his speech lives the woman whose soft voice
tames all beasts,
who feeds doves and scorpions alike.
He knows the secret name smoke carries in its own language.
He understands night and speaks its infinite epithets –

he knows the twelve words for waiting,
the three hundred diminutives of sad.
And through his voice
flows great calm
and the five tones that unite
thunder and raindrop.
His voice is the child at five
and the woman at eighty.
He comes to renew our world.

(Thrasymenes, poet and archon of the Greek colony of Phos in Mauretania)

XXVI

The Amanostoi who live north of the Hyperboreans crave originality.
Accordingly they destroy their houses each dawn in a mellow fire
they call "beginning". What occurs next is difficult to describe. Being
obliged to impress the word "novelty" on the surrounding air they gaze
dumbstruck a while at the poor effort made by the sun. Water, stone,
earth and fire all seem predictable building blocks. They shift from one
to the other, listlessly craving an effect that forever evades them. Each
morning seems the same. How they long for the old cultures when
each breath was prescribed by fixed rituals. How they yearn for those
ordered times when, instead of destroying their houses, men simply
destroyed each other.

(from Dio Cassius, *A true account of the circumnavigation of Europe
from Lusitanian Gades to the Chersonese Bosphorus*)

XXVII

We see the emblems in the land:
the south side of the city
where trees die off,
where a boy with a dog wanders far
along paths between sunken rice fields,
where a hot sky rains flakes of salt.

On the south side
puddles meander where roads die out.
The knife-grinder and the collector of rags
bend the horizon, distorting the world with their cries.
Myopic girls gather small coins for a sad time
and, if love comes, it must take its fragrance
from the racks of fish drying on the pebbles.

Birds desert us.
The swollen belly passes from the mother to the child.
On the south side when a life begins
a life ends.

(Poem written during the Second Great Hunger, Erycthemios, *Knowings*, Book II)

From Apocrypha Book IV

XXV

The blind horse knows the scent of the world.
Walk with it slowly.
Rest your hand on its mane
so you may know that nothing is endless.
There was a river that restored the tracks it erased.
There was a pebble not touched by any journeys
left behind for you alone
forgotten in the hands of the sky.

(Erycthemios, *Knowings*)

From Apocrypha Book V

I

Hanging upside down
perched in its own
Heaven
the cricket sings:
"I have eaten and am full.
This
is good."

Does it sing for us?
Possibly.
If we too have been touched all over by fire
If we have balanced for hours
on the infinite porosity of earth
and know what it's like
to be the casket of a time-beat
ticking away at metamorphosis
If at times our head and arms have wavered
like a delicate carapace flooded
by all the sky wants us to take in
If we can imagine the dryness of wind
caressing our black shell
all through the hot days
all through the fire of nights
when our eyes are beads of hard blackness
and our frame
breaks open to the homeless language of wind
If we can imagine ourselves
an assemblage of shell and flesh
scattered by the serene indifference of life

If we can call all this
happiness.

(from Irene Philologos, *A poetic journal of ten years in Boeotia*)

II

In the village of Ervan among the Oromati I was invited to a house
where one room is possessed by the force of absolute silence. In this
room numerous birdcages hang and inside them are pale, almost
transparent birds that have gradually shed all their colours in the
journey towards the invisible. The birds have lost all song and, from
the hollowness of their eyes, seem to have forgotten even the memory
of what song is. Only from time to time, in one corner of the room,
a bird beat itself against the bars of its cage, as if sensing an ancient
instinct that pain is the origin of sound.

(Porphyry the younger, *A journey from Ephesus to Nineveh*)

XIII
Responsibilities

to nightfall, always to carry an anchor bolted to my leg to make
    sure I will drown if thrown off a bridge by a wandering gymnast

to accept transmigration on whatever terms, even if as a patch of
    weeds used as a receptacle for kitchen slops, or as an orphaned duck
    crying his incontinence through the house, or the open hand of a leaf
    blown onto the path at twilight, its intricate web of veins receiving
    the entire weight of the sky

to the bricks that burn in the fireplace, to the kindling scattered in the
yard, to the re-invention of warmth

to the road beyond Paestum where the absolute chill ensures every
traveller will be lost

to the pure openness of your gaze even if in the faces of other women

to beds shared for a night or for years, and all the hollow places of the
world where there is no one but rain and time

to mice that congregate after nightfall, to the meticulous otters,
pigeons and a stork who stayed behind, wading through a river
that comes from the first days of the earth

to the spikes of the prickly-pear fruit, to appleblossoms

to an old woman dead now in a brothel on Samos

to the stones of the road, to a wooden bridge that slanted beyond the
furthest mountains, to a certain tree that measured the halfway
point from the village school to home

to count stars accurately, to avoid quarrels with birds, to leave the eagle
his right to distance and unpredictable vengeance

to make bread before dawn, to wash the feet of wanderers, to leave a
portion of each page blank that the Invisible may write their messages
to us, to each other

to the blazing fullness of midday entering the harbour at Alexandria,
to the fortress of Sardis where the walls glow pink with the last of
light failing

to a dark-eyed widow from Tyre and her three children, our few shared
days on the caravan to Yezd, her listless silence louder than the
snorting of horses, to whatever became of her

to the simple naming of losses, the grammar of obligations and the
wordless empty languages scattered in all places by beauty

to the wheat with its hunger for one more day of sun, to the grape
grown clouded and chill as mist across the fields at daybreak

to the crows of autumn, at all times to scan the shadows in the sunlit
pool, to know how gold is the last moment before brown,
to scavenge life from the bleak edge of survival

to the port of Agrigentum, to the olive groves on the hills
around Malea

to my sister who carried her three brothers across the roof of the
collapsing city

to the dead that they forgive us, to the unborn that the road be no
more broken

to a certain map of the world that showed how every place is infinite

to daybreak, thin trees and the winter sun

(Anonymous, from texts found in the Nestorian monastery in Bactria)

XXIV

When all that dreadful predictability
comes trudging up from the depths of the universe,
pleading "Say me. . . give voice to my long life",

how beautiful to hear the waterdrop
and its great tumble
from the broken gutter to the wooden floor.

What lies below us, what lies above us, suddenly the one sky.

(from Irene Philologos, *A poetic journal of ten years in Boeotia*

XXVI

From all the unbearable
uncertainty of Heaven
softly you enfold me.
I have no sea,
I have no space,
no sky to give you
trembling and wide enough.
Beloved unlooked-for,
the gaunt houses with the fear windows
are only as large
as all the days before now.

Three shadows cross your face,
three shadows trail
the soft curves of pain
my lips are stroking.

Frail
as if the air no longer held me,
I am the last leaf spinning
in an autumn sky.
Beloved all around me,
is this what happens when we enter
life's stillness,
is this the true knowing?

(Erycthemios, *Knowings*, the final poem)

XXVII
Jacarandas in Macabukro, almost spring

The tree of infinite veins,
though it blocks the sky,
gives us hope.
All its swirling outgrowths of bright yellow
are too fine for any destiny we know.
The wounded repetitions of its lowest branch,
however darkened, however it stubs itself out
in winter air,
are a rhythm the heart knows,
more beautiful than cherry trees
or the pale shade
of pink blossoms against snow.
For this is the god's shining
so high and endless
along the line of death.
Ungraspable –
but how could anyone imagine grasping –
this thin gold,

these fresh outbreaks of a denser
more fragrant pollen.
Under this canopy
ending anywhere
would be beginning.

(Omeros Eliseo, Poem 19 from *Nineteen Poems of Life and an Ode to Calm Temporarily Confused Ghosts*)

From Apocrypha Book VI

V

Born into the influential Chrysostomos clan, at nineteen Irene married her second cousin, Dimitri Philologos. Bitter feuds between rival families dominated the Empire on the death of Theodosius and Irene accompanied her husband into exile, following the machinations of the Blue court faction. Fearing a wave of popular support for the young Princess, the court faction renewed the edict of banishment after the death of her husband. Accustomed since childhood to wealth and prestige, in Boeotia Irene learned to live on millet soup and wild herbs, grateful for rain water where once she drank the finest wine. In a mountain village hearing only a local dialect incomprehensible to those from Byzantium, Irene displayed a tenacity undreamed of by her court enemies. Her writing, as she confessed, saved her inwardly, for there no Imperial edict could destroy her. In an age addicted to theological disputes, dull treatises and sycophantic histories, Irene's writing stands out. "A woman writing poetry in the middle of nowhere – how boorish, how monstrously antiquated – at best it will supply some paper for birds to nibble on", scoffed the Archbishop of Constantinople who presumed Irene would die soon enough, an exile in an uncouth mountain village. Her writings survived and were discovered in the eighteenth century in a monastery outside Deka Aghia. "Soon I will be dust", she wrote, "but the ants and the insects and the small things of the earth will remember me."

(Preface to a planned edition of the poems of Irene Philologos, from the papers of Dr Antoine Lemesurier, assistant curator, The Secret Library Trust of Lower Egypt)

VI

Crouched by a lone fire
in the wide country
where the world has vanished.

~o~

Across the lake
they are burning holes in the sky –
tender sparks
twist upward into night.

~o~

Learning to look at shadows
detached from whatever they might once
have accompanied:

scruffy strays
liberated
into the carelessness of beauty.

~o~

In the pure open
a great steady fire caresses each being
with its slowly diminishing touch

from layer to layer
gradually out to the white stars that speak back

~o~

The small bare table
where the bread has not yet been laid
speaks as a lover makes love:
entirely there.

~o~

The fish have been passed through a net –
sifting their jagged loneliness
into a paste of bone.

~o~

Art, like love,
permits us to fall into it
to discover our own falling.

(Irene Philologos, from *A poetic journal of ten years in Boeotia*)

IX

It is easy to believe there is another language always present at the
edge of hearing, some slight, altogether bewildering shift in what we
thought the finite reality called music, a colour no one has seen yet,
familiar perhaps to some other people but hidden entirely from us,
words with a nuance another tribe would grasp immediately but, to us,
forever incomprehensible, something that could have lifted the whole
of our lives into another truth, another intensity of joy and coherence
and depth, the lost key that would redeem so many wasted years, so
much bitterness. It was always so close and simple, like the fragrance
of a certain sweet burnt on windy nights when the temperature drops
to a level almost but not quite that of snow and the streets hold sound

in a different way. For such things enlist no deities. Their truth is all in their simplicity, the richness they give to living, the richness that assures us living is always just a beginning.

~ø~

Made of the softest wood and manifesting at every step how perishable it is, the star-stair winds upwards and upwards from the dirt floor of the marketplace, a crowded chaotic space where pigs roam at random, beggars and thieves are always jostling against wide-eyed strangers, small girls cradle baby sisters. The tower that houses the star-stair is a thin soaring structure of perhaps 29 or 66 floors, reaching almost to the clouds. The young child named the Goddess of Dawn is said to live there at the summit and on a few occasions has been seen by visitors. All the tower's passageways are remarkably small, designed perhaps for five year olds while adults need to hunch over tightly to make their way up the stairs. The intervening floors are said to contain the world in miniature.

Every three years the building is first emptied, then burnt to the ground so that a new offering to the sky can be created – either because the wood perishes or because of a fear that magic slips from everything faster than water glides through the fingers of our hands. A new child is then found to be the Goddess. The mysterious thousand rooms that symbolize the world must be shaped once more. In this way the sea that goes away comes back once more.

~ø~

Returning by boat from Egypt and the Kingdoms of lower Africa I felt listless and ill at ease to be once more on familiar Italian soil. Then in the nightmarkets of Brundisium I came across an at first scarcely intelligible treatise on geography. Carefully inscribed on its front cover was its date of publication: MMMXCV: but from what era or what land?

Slowly I began to accumulate a library of books from the future. In them I read of a sequence of world devastations, of the disappearance of the human species not once but several times and, connected to this phenomenon, of the philosopher Irenaeus of Chalcedony who taught that the chief error of the ancients from Socrates to Aristotle, from the cynics to the malcontents, was to imagine the ethical word belonged exclusively to man and not to life. "All imagine", he says at one point on page 77 of a vanishing treatise *On the Interpretation of Sand*, "as if individually they would die yet somehow the human species, the human word would survive forever. Let us suppose, instead, it is life not mankind that survives. Let us imagine that the ethical, the beautiful survives forever despite – or because of? – our perishing. Suppose one day in the wider trajectories of the cosmos the ethical, the beautiful will summon back snails, hillsides dotted with yellow flowers and birds with gracious wings, and perhaps, out of a lingering yearning for what passion brings, a young man and woman in their most intense lovemaking, their faces opened entirely to each other as if in those hours they could read in one unbroken gaze all that life utters, the infinite scripture of the world there in the tender curve of a beloved's face. In that scripture is the totality of surrender, a rippling outwards, what does not seek to clutch but to give."

~ø~

We were on the highest terrace where the image of the sea glittered in a wide endless sweep. I do not know how long it was since the last flight of birds had gone, tracing their way beyond the horizon of the visible. Certainly for what seemed an immense trajectory of time nothing stirred or changed beyond the narrow world of the terrace with our few movements of the head or an arm, our slight leaning towards or away from each other, perhaps the momentary gesture of touching a plate of food only to draw back from it. The woman who sat beside me moved forward at one moment as if to kiss me only to draw back, just as our hands, though exquisitely shaping the same air, remained separate. I do not know her age exactly but she seemed very young and kept slipping backwards into the unguarded instant of being an adolescent, almost a girl, ready to love and go on to marry, have children, while I, whatever my real age, drifted steadily into being an old man, half paralysed, my face creased and life-worn, with only a few brief years left. It was a transformation she sensed in me over which I had no control. But a delicacy of absolute longing and stillness held us enraptured for those hours that were at once, though neither our words nor our gestures said this, one unbroken outpouring of love and leave-taking. For so many years, the long years of bitter aloneness, I hated myself for this shame, this desertion by life when life had summoned me. Now at the ending of days I sense only the beauty of her face, the mutual truth of blessing.

~ø~

Facing the dark and naming it, I remind myself, doesn't mean wanting to live there. The beauty of the earth is seamless and obeys no logos. It prepares its own remedies – the dream cure, the writing cure, restoration through music. So the return of the sea follows the charter of the moon and tenderness lets life flow back. Inwardly we walk the earth as many people. Outwardly in dimensions visible and invisible our speech, when it has left demands and grievances behind, continues

(from Lucius of Ocampo, *Interrogating a lost life – notes towards an autobiographic philosophy*)

XXVII

There are words –
we don't know what they are –
and summers –
we don't know if we'll get there –
and doorways left open
into bright courtyards
and an arrangement that looks like life
though the water is rising past our ankles.
Through all the thirteen tiers of the serried hillside,
sleep, we can't find you.

The distances are what they are:
magical.

(Irene Philologos, from *A poetic journal of ten years in Boeotia*)

From Apocrypha Book VII

V
Ballad of the Three Marias

This little turtle has no sea —
place him gently in a cart,
let the cart set out
into the land where there is only stone and sand,
let it roll over dry earth, across boulders, shattered ground,
out to an open space
where the sky will take pity and send him a turtle-sized sea.

Three Marias appear on the road,
three Marias out walking
looking for the river that was.
Where the river should be
only stone and dry grass.
They say, "Where is this river?
Where are the fish that swam here,
the reeds that wrapped and twined around our feet
when we came here to wash and taste the coolness?"

One gives a handkerchief to the other —
it passes through the third Mary's body.
One gives a comb to the other —
a butterfly flutters out
from the opening in the forehead.

The three Marias are sitting on three stones.
Each has forgotten the name of her lost son.

Above the sand

spirit fish spin in the rivers of air.
A fish knows how to carry coolness deep inside its body,
how water glides
even when it can't be seen.
The spirit fish are whispering the names of all the stars.

A stone shines where the water goes on living.
The son travels the bright skies
towards the birthplace of names.

(from an Armenian songbook found in the Coptic library at Erzerum)

VI

How do you live in a country that is travelling backwards? Each day it
loses more of itself. Year by year its leaders strive to remove whatever
elements of justice or compassion its people had slowly acquired. It
prides itself on destruction and believes every reality can be renamed.
So the great vanishing grows.

(Leonidas the self-exiled, *The Grey Notebook*)

XIII
Burial Chamber

They come drifting towards us as stars come drifting across skies. They
illuminate and darken at the same time. They perceive the blackened,
the eradicated portions of their bodies. They perceive an earth where
blackened, eradicated eyes and voices speak, answering each other
across the curve of night. Above, a few stars, stubbed-out, abolished,
still travel their own space, counterbalancing the earth's weight.

Our speech is a babble, a false summoning, wordshapes erected as an anti-tombstone over the great killing

Two chairs sit opposite me – it could be they are waiting for the King and Queen of the dark – they look almost Minoan. The head-dresses that grace the absent shoulders will come later. Behind them a window looks out on our small share of the infinite. I assume that sooner or later the occupants will arrive. I am not sure, though, that any person could quite replace the luminous power of emptiness. No matter how strange or how monstrous, they would look too much like ourselves.

(fragment from *The Secret Book of Infinite Space*, old Persian text found in the Nestorian monastery of Tabriz)

XXVII

A speck of peppercorn
stuck in the corner of my mouth –
there, beyond the last wine and the sweets,
still tasting of the harsh earth,
offering me the heart of distant pathways
to chew on.

* * *

An implausible winter burrows a tunnel
between your hand and mine.
Beloved, our life-battered bodies
merge in a prayer of white beginnings.
Threaded wands of trees like the hairs of your pubis
tremble in the air's cool wonder.

Beauty like the soft plains of your flesh
lies far away, an exiled land,
lies right here too
under the dream protection of my hand.

*   *   *

The slowed-down world
glitters carefully in the small stream
where yesterday's mud
puts down roots.
Everything grows in the palm of something else.
Only our wounds face the night sky
with the fierce simplicity of their barbarous tongues.

(Flavinius of Cappadocia, *The roads of the troubled sky: fragmentaria from eight years in the slave colony of Neapolis*)

XXVIII

Travelling in a caravan towards the World Capital where the Great King had invited him to speak at a symposium on the four elements, the philosopher let his mind drift from topic to topic, seeking an adequate response to present. Already they had crossed many lands and for some time now the unbounded sea ran alongside his meditations. The philosopher wanted to think of how we are in the world. The words "violence" and "loss" seemed essential to him, the words "cherishing" and "holding back". The sea the caravan journeyed beside stretched all the way to the island of dogs, the island where dogs cast aside by sailors had established their own community – a space little more than a sandbank where an immense loneliness ranged for here lived the dogs who had been cast out by humans.

On the sandbank where the dogs lived the wild closeness of the stars generated the music of grief. Eventually the resonances of the music sealed the island off and, like many things that become too strong for human consciousness, it flickered inside and outside time, appearing and disappearing across the void, indifferent to the changing names of the millennia.

He wondered in turn what would become of the people without dogs, those who sailed on to make new lands abandoning everything once cherished. Deciding that speech and closeness robbed them of marketable time, they developed a thing language to replace the old creature languages. Instead of talking, they held up objects and compared one with another, and so stillness was banished to the remotest distance.

(from Lucius of Ocampo, *Interrogating a lost life – notes towards an autobiographic philosophy*)

XXIX
Summoning the Angel

I read words jumbled out of Scrabble sets
        and they speak to me absolutely.
The most beautiful poems appear in the tender spaces of marigolds
        left to breathe freely between railway tracks.
I have a taste for the burnt leaves that fall in an autumn of cinders.
In the aisle for lost causes two squabbling children struggling with
food wrappers perform the most elaborate ballet, the poignant ferocity
of their fingers crumbling the world's textures.
A man examines the map of an exploding tree and walks for five days
        seeking the almond of sleep that is his double.

Across the earth a little light and a little light is extinguished.

I open my terrified arms into a stillness I have never known, at home
with my cousins the ants and the twenty four stepsisters
who address all the stars by their first names.
Brown blood spurts a small voice in the centre of each hand.
The universe invades me.
Breaking waves pass effortlessly through my forehead, their
        uninterrupted surge the kiss that peels me open.
My middle name is "River that never was".

In the estimation of crows all that is blue is possessable, the white
        eyes of the fearful an affront.
Starting from nowhere, a rough sand causeway bends, twists and
        heads off into the distance towards the faint outline of spires.
On this day I am embraced by deer who recognise buildings as forests
        that once went astray.

(among the final notebooks of W O'S, this appears to be a loose adaptation
of the lost poem "An Ode to calm temporarily confused ghosts" by Omeros
Eliseo)

Acknowledgements

Several of these poems have appeared in *Bluepepper, Mascara, Meanjin, PAN, Southerly, The Sun Herald, The Stinging Fly* (Ireland), *La Traductière* (France), *Shearsman* (UK).

"Summer Day" and "Towns in the Great Desert (2)" were published in *Best Australian Poems 2010* edited by Robert Adamson.

"Clarity of the Word" was published in *Best Australian Poetry 2011* edited by John Tranter.

"The Guardian Angel" was published in *Best Australian Poetry 2012* edited by John Tranter.

"(an afternoon with you)" was published in *Best Australian Love Poems* (edited by Mark Tredinnick, Black Inc Press, 2013)

"Towns in the Great Desert (11)", "Fig Tree", "The Tree's Ambition", and "Nocturne (1)" were published in French translation in *Livre d'Or de Struga, Volume 1, Poètes du monde*, Paris, 2011.

"In the Sleep of the Riverbed", originally published as "The riverbed that marks the edge of the mountains adds an extra curve to its journey to converse with the ghost of Federico García Lorca" and "Reading Borges, Late at Night and Imagining Buenos Aires" were first published in *Reading Borges* (Picaro Press, 2007).

"Reading Max Jacob in Taichung", "Nocturne (10)" and "The Tree's Ambition" were published in *Small Wonder: an anthology of prose poems and microfictions*, edited by Linda Godfrey and Julie Chevalier, Spineless Wonders, 2012.

"Towns in the Great Desert (11)" and "The Banker Who Owns the Stars" were published in *Here Not There*, edited by Judith Beveridge and Carolyn Rickett, Puncher and Wattmann, 2012.

Notes

p 175 APEIRON ZENODOKHEIO: The words are a shortened, fractured version (as for a makeshift sign) of a phrase by George Seferis in his poem "Thrush": "ena aperanto zenodokheio"(a limitless hotel). In the translation by Edmund Keeley and Philip Sherrard the passage reads:

> When the architect's finished, they* change,
> they frown or smile or even grow stubborn
> with those who stayed behind, with those who went away
> with others who'd come back if they could
> or others who disappeared, now the world's become
> a limitless hotel.

[* houses]

George Seferis, *Collected Poems 1924 – 1955,* translated by Keeley and Sherrard, Jonathan Cape, 1969, p 312/313

www.ingramcontent.com/pod-product-compliance
Lightning Source LLC
Chambersburg PA
CBHW030823090426
42737CB00009B/853